SCHOLASTIC

SUMMER EXPRESS ™

NEW YORK • TORONTO • LONDON • AUCKLAND • SYDNEY
MEXICO CITY • NEW DELHI • HONG KONG • BUENOS AIRES

Authors: Frankie Long, M.Ed. & Leland Graham, Ph.D.
Cover design by Brian LaRossa
Cover photo © MediaBakery
Interior illustrations by Teresa Anderko and Mike Moran

ISBN: 978-0-545-30590-7

3 4 5 6 7 8 9 10   08   17 16 15 14 13

Table of Contents

Dear Parent:

Congratulations! You hold in your hands an exceptional educational tool that will give your child a head start into the coming school year.

Inside this book, you will find one hundred practice pages that will help your middle schooler review and learn math, reading, writing, grammar, vocabulary, and so much more! *Summer Express* is divided into ten weeks, with two practice pages for each day of the week, Monday to Friday. However, feel free to use the pages in any order that your child likes. Here are a few features you will find inside:

- Suggestions for fun, creative **learning activities** you can do with your child each week.

- A weekly **journal entry sheet** so that your middle schooler can record his or her goals for the week as well as respond to the journal entries.

- A **recommended reading list** of age-appropriate books that you and your middle schooler can read throughout the summer.

- A **certificate of completion** to celebrate your middle schooler's accomplishments.

We hope you and your middle schooler will have fun as you work together to complete *Summer Express!*

Enjoy!
The Editors

Terrific Tips for Using This Book

1 Decide on a good time of day for your child to work on the activities. You may want your child to do them around mid-morning or early afternoon when he or she is not too tired.

2 Make sure your middle schooler has all the supplies he or she needs, such as a ruler, pencils, erasers, and markers. Set aside a special place for your child to work.

3 At the beginning of each week, discuss how many minutes a day your child plans to read. We recommend that a student entering the eighth grade read 45 minutes to 1 hour a day, including any time spent on required summer reading and projects.

4 Reward your middle schooler's efforts with free time for video games, texting, or his or her favorite pastime. Set a goal for the week and a reasonable reward for achieving the goal.

5 Encourage your middle schooler to complete each worksheet, but do not force the issue. While you may want to ensure that your child succeeds, it is also important to maintain a positive and relaxed attitude toward school and learning.

6 After you have given your middle schooler a few minutes to look over the practice pages, ask what his or her plan is for completing the pages. Hearing the explanation aloud can provide insight into his or her thinking processes. At this point, you can decide if your child can complete the work independently or needs guidance. If he or she needs support, present choices about which family member he or she might work with. Providing choices can help boost confidence and encourage your child to take more ownership of the work to be done.

7 When your child has finished the workbook, why not present the certificate of completion on page 143 at a family gathering or dinner at his or her favorite restaurant?

Skill-Building Activities for Any Time

The following activities are designed to complement the ten weeks of practice pages in this book. These activities do not take more than a few minutes to complete. Use them to turn otherwise idle time into productive time—for example, standing in a line at a store or waiting at the bus stop. It's a great way to practice key skills and have fun together at the same time.

Finding Real-Life Connections

One of the reasons for schooling is to help children function in the real world, to empower them with the abilities they truly need. Help your child develop these real-life skills by enlisting his or her help with reading a map, following a recipe, checking grocery receipts, calculating a restaurant tip, and so on. By applying reading, writing, science, and math skills in relevant and practical ways, he or she will better understand the importance of these skills.

An Eye for Patterns

A red-brick sidewalk, a beaded necklace, a Sunday newspaper—all show evidence of structure and organization. You can help your child recognize a variety of structure or types of organization by observing and talking about patterns they see. The ability to identify patterns is a skill shared by effective readers, writers, scientists, and mathematicians.

Journals as Learning Tools

Journal writing reinforces reading comprehension, but it also helps your middle schooler develop skills in many academic areas as well. A journal can simply be a spiral notebook, a composition notebook, or sheets of paper stapled together. Your middle schooler will be writing and/or drawing in the journal to complement the practice pages completed each week. The journal provides another tool for monitoring the progress of newly learned skills and practicing those that need improvement. Before moving on to another set of practice pages, take a few minutes to read and discuss that week's journal entries with your child.

Promote Reading at Home

◆ Practice what you preach! You and your middle schooler should both read for pleasure, whether you like reading science-fiction novels or do-it-yourself magazines. Reading should not always be work. **Sometimes we should read just for fun!** Keeping reading materials around the house encourages you to read in front of your child and demonstrates that reading is an activity you enjoy.

◆ Set aside a family reading time. By designating a reading time each week, your family is assured an opportunity to discuss what everyone is reading. For example, you might share a funny quote from an article, or your middle schooler can tell you his or her favorite part of a story. The key is to **make a family tradition of reading—and sharing what you've read**.

◆ **Make a family collection of reading materials** easily accessible by everyone. Designate a specific place for library books and post the return date. This idea will help prevent library fines. Keep reading materials fresh and interesting by buying used books, swapping books and magazines with friends and neighbors, as well as checking out books from the library.

Skills Review and Practice

Educators have established learning standards for math and language arts. Listed below are some of the important skills covered in *Summer Express* that will help your middle schooler review and prepare for the coming school year so that he or she is ready to meet these learning standards.

Math

7th Grade Skills to Review

- reviewing basic operations with whole numbers, fractions, and decimals
- applying formulas to find measurements of plane figures
- understanding the location of points on a coordinate grid on any of the four quadrants
- applying a variety of strategies to solve problems requiring algebraic formulas
- evaluating expressions and formulas
- devising a plan to solve a problem
- applying a variety of strategies to solve two-step equations with one variable
- using estimation to determine the reasonableness of answers
- applying concepts and procedures from probability and statistics
- reviewing order of operations

Skills to Practice for 8th Grade

- devising a plan to solve any type of problem
- interpreting different forms of data
- studying Pythagoras and his theorem
- performing basic operations on algebraic expressions
- identifying rays, lines, end points, line segments, vertices, and angles
- understanding and applying the procedures for simplifying single variable expressions

Language Arts

7th Grade Skills to Review

- identifying the correct use of parts of speech
- improving use of punctuation, capitalization, and spelling
- recognizing and differentiating different types of sentences
- demonstrating proof of reading comprehension
- understanding and applying knowledge of text components to comprehend text
- reading new information or following directions
- using clauses, phrases, gerunds, and infinitives correctly
- understanding root words, synonyms, antonyms, and homophones
- identifying commonly used foreign words and phrases
- gathering information from a variety of sources

Skills to Practice for 8th Grade

- knowing and using the different types of sentences
- demonstrating knowledge of correct sentence structure
- using correct capitalization and punctuation
- distinguishing between clauses, phrases, and sentences
- differentiating between independent and dependent clauses
- differentiating between simple, compound, complex, and compound-complex sentences
- recognizing English words derived from Greek roots
- identifying common phrases and terms from other languages used in English
- identifying a topic and gathering information from a variety of sources
- reading information for a variety of purposes
- identifying and using different styles of writing: persuasive, expository, or narrative
- determining best word choice based on context

Helping Your Middle Schooler Get Ready: Week 1

These are the skills your middle schooler will be working on this week.

Math
- basic operations
- coordinate points
- money word problems

Reading
- reading for information

Writing
- creating an outline
- descriptive writing

Vocabulary
- context clues

Grammar
- nouns
- clauses: dependent and independent

Here are some activities you and your middle schooler might enjoy.

Creating a Teen Retreat Your middle schooler is about to enter eighth grade and the "real" teen years. A great summer activity that will make him or her feel more grown-up is a bedroom update. Have your child make a list of what changes he or she would like to make in the room. Spend some time together clipping photos from magazines and catalogs, gathering fabric and paint samples, and anything else that seems interesting. Collect and edit until the dream room and the family budget are a match. Before starting, have your teen make a floor plan, and then do some preliminary online pricing for paint or other supplies. Encourage him or her to rearrange the furniture and decide together what should be stored away.

Set a Summer's End Goal Suggest that your child set some goals for the end of the summer—perhaps becoming a better cook or tackling a new sport. Help your child come up with a plan for success.

Your middle schooler might enjoy reading one of the following books:

The Incredible Journey
by Sheila Burnford

James and the Giant Peach
by Roald Dahl

Light, Sound & Electricity
by Kirsteen Rogers et. al.

Summer Goals:
1. Complete required summer reading and projects.
2. Explore a new genre.
3. Learn a new sport.
4. Expand baking and cooking skills.

My Week at a Glance

Use this page to set goals and make journal entries.

Goals for Monday_____

_____

Journal: Imagine and describe a perfect summer day. What would you do? Who would you do it with? Where would you go?

_____

_____

_____

_____

Goals for Tuesday_____

_____

Goals for Wednesday_____

_____

Journal: Imagine you could be a character in your favorite video game. Who would you choose to be? What would be special about the new you?

_____

_____

_____

_____

Goals for Thursday_____

_____

Goals for Friday_____

_____

Journal: Mark Twain once said, "To get the full value of a joy, you must have somebody to divide it with." What do you think he meant by that? Do you agree or disagree? Why?

_____

_____

_____

_____

Lost at Camp

Trace a path from the Parking Lot to the Campfire Circle by following eight correctly written equations. Avoid ones with mistakes.

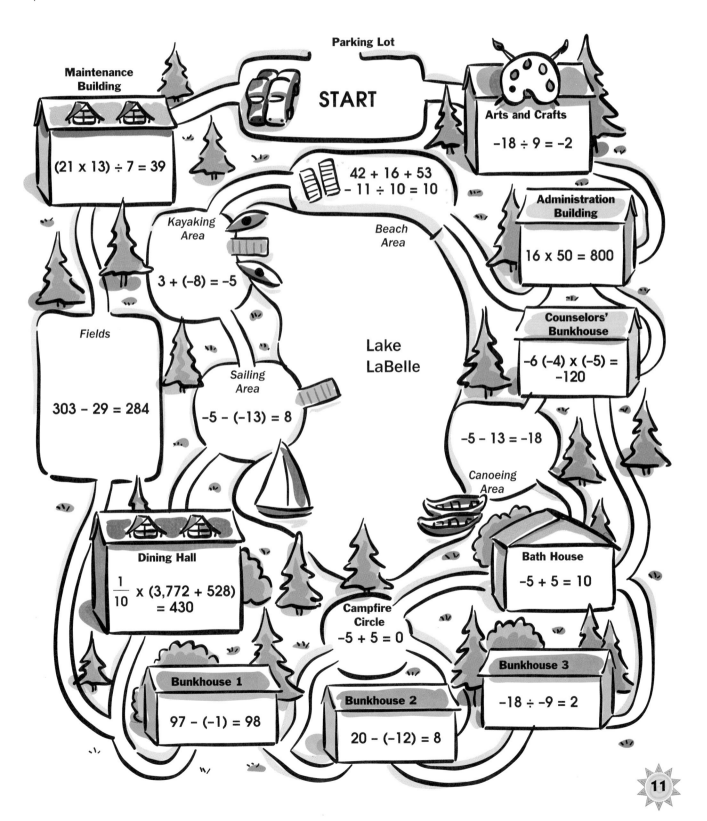

Parking Lot

START

Maintenance Building
$(21 \times 13) \div 7 = 39$

Arts and Crafts
$-18 \div 9 = -2$

$42 + 16 + 53 - 11 \div 10 = 10$

Administration Building
$16 \times 50 = 800$

Kayaking Area
$3 + (-8) = -5$

Beach Area

Counselors' Bunkhouse
$-6 \, (-4) \times (-5) = -120$

Fields

Lake LaBelle

Sailing Area
$-5 - (-13) = 8$

$303 - 29 = 284$

$-5 - 13 = -18$

Canoeing Area

Dining Hall
$\frac{1}{10} \times (3{,}772 + 528) = 430$

Bath House
$-5 + 5 = 10$

Campfire Circle
$-5 + 5 = 0$

Bunkhouse 1
$97 - (-1) = 98$

Bunkhouse 2
$20 - (-12) = 8$

Bunkhouse 3
$-18 \div -9 = 2$

11

It's Only Proper!

 A **common noun** names any person, place, thing, or idea. A **proper noun** names a particular person, place, thing, or idea. Here are some examples of common and proper nouns. Common nouns are not capitalized, but proper nouns are.

Common Nouns	Proper Nouns
city	Atlanta
river	Mississippi River
poet	Maya Angelou
street	Main Street
organization	Boy Scouts of America

Read the following sentences. Underline the common nouns and circle the proper nouns.

1. Monaco is the second smallest country in Europe.

2. Brittany and her two best friends live on Washington Street.

3. The American Red Cross brings aid to people during disasters.

4. The United States is a democratic country.

5. William Butler Yeats wrote beautiful poetry!

6. He wrote the poem, "The Lake Isle of Innisfree."

7. This Irish land must be quite special to the poet.

8. The place of which Yeats wrote is near Sligo, Ireland.

9. The sights beyond the lake include views of the Lough Gill Mountains.

10. The Hazelwood Sculpture Trail is close to the lake.

11. The United Nations is in New York City.

12. Nathan is an excellent guitarist.

13. Australia is the smallest continent.

14. Lincoln Avenue is our town's busiest street.

15. Josh and Molly are cousins.

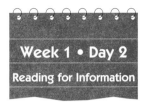

Hatshepsut

Throughout the long history of Ancient Egypt, its rulers, or **pharaohs**, were almost always men. But one woman did succeed in becoming pharaoh. Hatshepsut was a princess married to a pharaoh. When her husband died, her 10-year-old stepson should have become the pharaoh. But Hatshepsut saw a chance to seize power. She claimed the boy was too young to rule and demanded to be named his co-ruler.

To be sure people saw her as pharaoh, Hatshepsut had to dress the part. She adopted all of the **accoutrements** of a pharaoh: the headdress, clothes, and even the fake beard worn by all of Egypt's pharaohs.

Hatshepsut not only looked the part of a powerful leader, she acted it. Historians characterize her reign as a time of peace and prosperity for Egypt. She oversaw the creation of many great works of art, restored religious temples, and, most important, organized trade networks. She ruled Egypt for 20 years.

After her death, Hatshepsut's stepson, Thuthmose III, came to power. Unfortunately, he attempted to erase Hatshepsut from history. He began destroying everything he could find with her image or name on it. Despite Thuthmose III's efforts, some artifacts remained for researchers to unearth. Archaeologists found evidence of Hatshepsut's rule, and today we know many things about this successful female pharaoh.

Answer the following questions.

1. **Hatshepsut was—**
   A. an archaeologist.
   B. a pharaoh.
   C. an Egyptian model.
   D. a historian.

2. **A pharaoh is—**
   A. always male.
   B. an archaeologist.
   C. the name for a ruler of Ancient Egypt.
   D. a princess.

3. **What happened first?**
   A. Hatshepsut restored temples.
   B. Thuthmose III came to power.
   C. Researchers uncovered her story.
   D. Hatshepsut became pharaoh.

4. **Hatshepsut's reign is characterized by—**
   A. peace and prosperity.
   B. uprisings against the throne.
   C. destruction of Thuthmose III's image.
   D. unrelenting drought and famine.

5. **Accoutrements refer to—**
   A. great works of art.
   B. a successor to the throne.
   C. clothing and accessories.
   D. acts of royal vandalism.

6. **When Thuthmose III claimed the throne—**
   A. an age of peace and prosperity began.
   B. he tried to erase any sign of Hatshepsut.
   C. she became the first female pharaoh.
   D. he decided not to wear a false beard.

7. **Hatshepsut's story was discovered by—**
   A. researchers.
   B. a pharaoh.
   C. Thuthmose III.
   D. her husband.

8. **To look like a pharaoh, Hatshepsut—**
   A. learned a sacred dance.
   B. studied in Greece under philosophers.
   C. decided to retire after 20 years.
   D. wore special clothes and a fake beard.

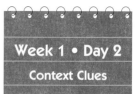

Vocabulary Building: Context Clues

You can sometimes find the meaning of an unfamiliar word by using context clues, or the words or phrases around the word.

Using context clues, underline the correct word to complete each sentence.

1. **The sad news made Malik feel very (somber, elated).**

2. **During a hectic day, reading a book is a welcome (interlude, intermediate) for Carmen.**

3. **Because of her (persistence, resistance), Leticia finally learned to drive a car.**

4. **Janie loves vegetables more than anything, so she (avoids, prefers) cheeseburgers.**

5. **Mario improved his (endurance, resistance) during swim meets by practicing every day.**

6. **Jonathan's track team drank gallons of lemonade after their track meet because they were so (dehydrated, depopulated).**

Complete each sentence below by choosing a word from the word box that makes sense in the blank. Be sure to use the context clues in the sentence to help you.

| erode | aerospace | hydrant | manipulate | participate |

1. **In case of fire at your house, would you be able to direct the fire department to the nearest**

   _____?

2. **An airplane pilot has to _____ the controls in order to fly the plane.**

3. **Wind and running water continually _____, or wear away, soil and rocks.**

4. **Eliot cannot _____ in sports after school because he must go home to take care of his brother.**

5. **Because Yoko is planning an _____ career, she is studying about the earth's atmosphere.**

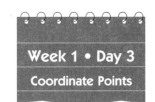
A Graph Puzzle

Use the graph on the next page. Follow the directions to complete this puzzle.

1. **Plot each ordered pair below, and then connect all the points with a straight line segment.**

(4, 1)	(−10, 7)	$(-7\frac{1}{2}, -3)$
(8, 0)	$(-9\frac{1}{2}, 8\frac{1}{2})$	(−6, −1)
(14, 3)	(−14, 6)	(−4, −1)
(20, 10)	$(-15, 4\frac{1}{2})$	(−6, −7)
(9, 4)	$(-16, 1\frac{1}{2})$	$(-12\frac{1}{2}, -11)$
(6, 4)	(−15, 0)	(−11, −11)
(2, 7)	$(-13\frac{1}{2}, 2)$	(−5, −9)
(−2, 8)	(−8, −1)	(1, −3)
(−6, 7)	(−7, −1)	(4, 1)
(−10, 4)	$(-8\frac{1}{2}, -3)$	**Plot this ordered pair. Do not connect.**
(−13, 6)	(−7, −4)	(−14, 4)

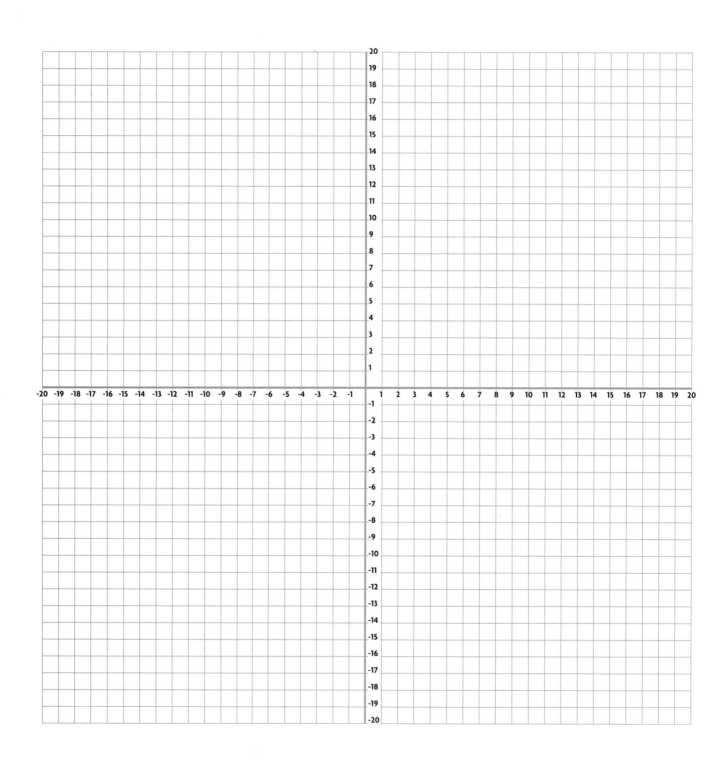

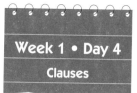

Dependent and Independent Clauses

A **clause** is a group of related words. A clause has both a subject and a predicate. There are two types of clauses, independent and dependent.

Independent Clause—An independent clause can stand alone as a sentence.
Example: We walked to the park last night.

Dependent Clause—A dependent clause cannot stand alone as a sentence.
Example: When we checked the cookies in the oven.

Read each clause. Write **I** for an independent clause. Write **D** for a dependent clause.

_____ 1. Because you enjoy pizza so much.

_____ 2. After you have finished the yard work.

_____ 3. The library book that you want is on the third shelf.

_____ 4. Although she enjoys playing the piano.

_____ 5. There must be a way to solve this problem.

_____ 6. I am too busy to go to the movies tonight.

_____ 7. Since they left here to go to San Francisco.

_____ 8. Eduardo waved to his friends.

Read each sentence. Circle each independent clause and underline each dependent clause.

9. As the population increases, the world faces a shortage of fresh water.

10. We ordered spaghetti, which everyone in the family likes.

11. While my brothers were working during the summer, I went to summer school.

12. Please show me the book that you read this summer.

Money Saving Coupons

Read each coupon. Then, solve the word problems.

1. **The dance team is having a sleepover Friday evening before the team's car washing fundraiser. Meredith found a donut special at Dizzy Donuts for $4.60 per dozen. She purchased six dozen donuts. Her total bill for the donuts was**

   $____________

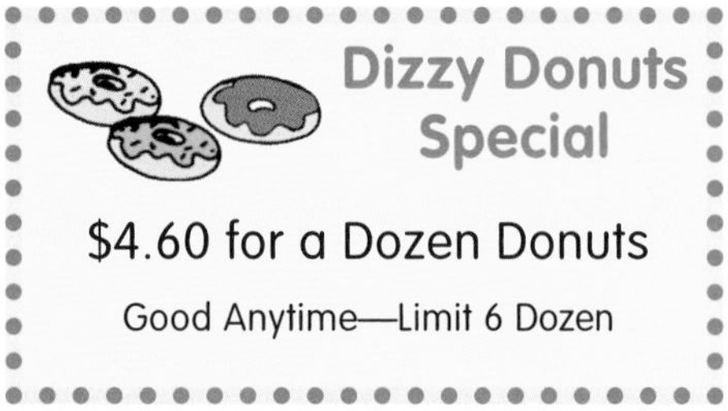
Dizzy Donuts Special
$4.60 for a Dozen Donuts
Good Anytime—Limit 6 Dozen

2. **Best Ever chocolate chip cookies are $3.79 per bag at the Super Special Market. Super Special doubles the value of coupons on Tuesdays. Sue is shopping on Tuesday and buys two packages of cookies. What is the cost of cookies, not including taxes?**

   $____________

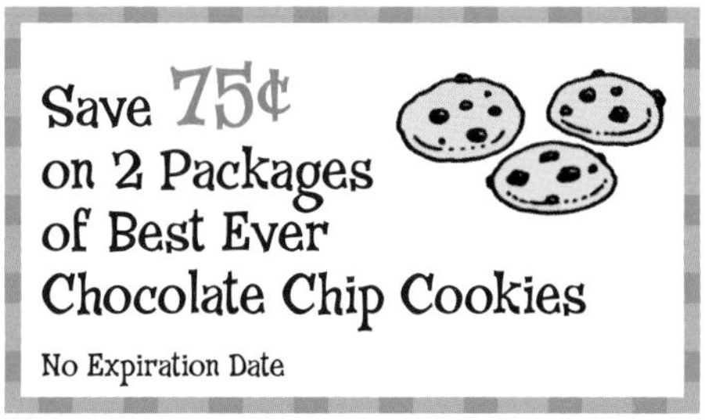
Save 75¢
on 2 Packages
of Best Ever
Chocolate Chip Cookies
No Expiration Date

3. **Hotter Than Hot costs $1.79 per bottle. On a triple-value coupon day, what would be the cost before taxes per bottle?**

   $____________

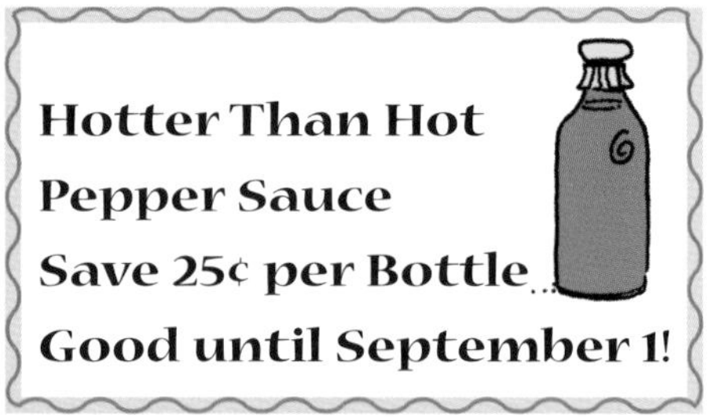
Hotter Than Hot
Pepper Sauce
Save 25¢ per Bottle...
Good until September 1!

4. **The Testa family had lunch at Osvaldo's. Each of the four family members had three tacos at a cost of $2.50 each. Mr. and Mrs. Testa each had iced tea for $1.95, and the girls each had a soft drink for the same price. What was their check before taxes and tip, but after the discount? Read the coupon carefully!**

   $____________

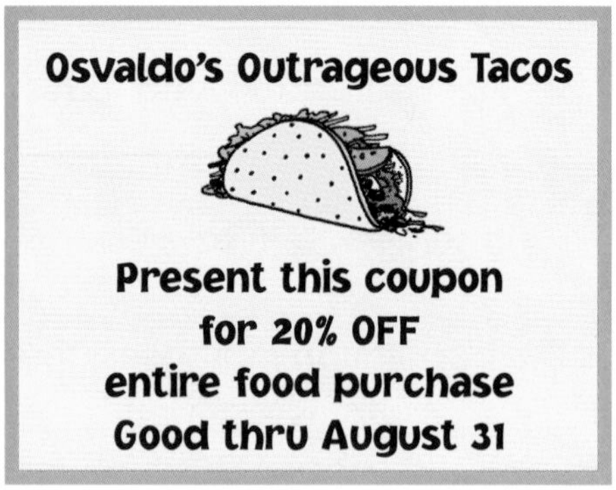
Osvaldo's Outrageous Tacos
Present this coupon
for 20% OFF
entire food purchase
Good thru August 31

5. **John's Car Care Center normally charges $39.95 for the special oil change. According to the coupon, what will the discounted price be? (Round to the nearest penny.)**

   $____________

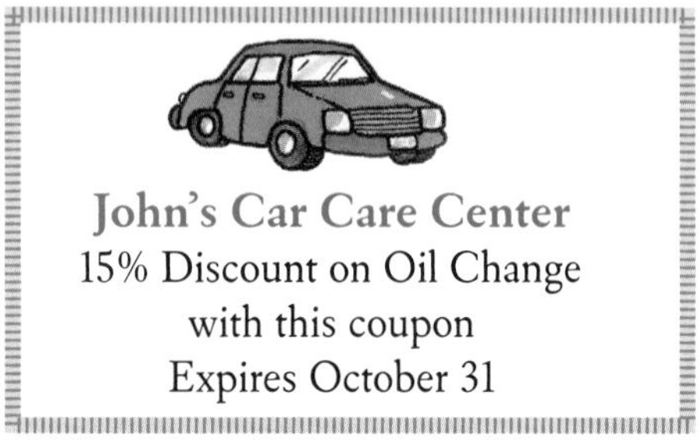
John's Car Care Center
15% Discount on Oil Change
with this coupon
Expires October 31

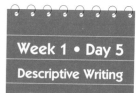

Descriptive Writing Prompt

Think about the last time you attended a special event, such as a baseball game, a concert, a trip to an amusement park, or a field trip. Follow the steps below to write a descriptive paragraph about the event.

1. **Select a topic for your special event:**_____

2. **Use this graphic organizer to brainstorm ways to describe the event using your five senses.**

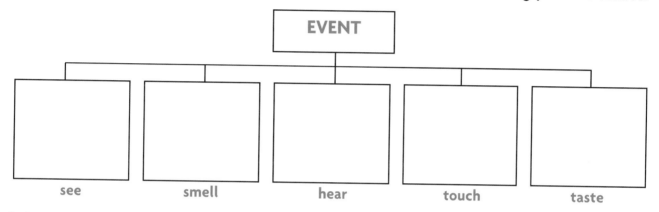

3. **Make an outline, using your ideas from above. Include descriptions related to at least three senses and two supporting details for each point.**

_____
Title

I _____

  A. _____

  B. _____

  C. _____

II _____

  A. _____

  B. _____

  C. _____

III _____

  A. _____

  B. _____

19

Descriptive Writing

Next, write a draft on a separate sheet of paper based on the outline that you created. Edit the first draft and recopy your final paragraph on the lines below. Be sure to share your paragraph with your family.

_____

Title

_____

_____

_____

_____

_____

_____

_____

_____

_____

_____

_____

_____

_____

These are the skills your middle schooler will be working on this week.

Math
- mixed fractions
- order of operations
- geometry: tangrams

Reading
- reading for information
- reading for details

Writing
- combining sentences
- expository writing

Vocabulary
- word work: degree of meaning

Grammar
- capitalization and punctuation

Here are some activities you and your middle schooler might enjoy.

A Daily Life Skill Challenge your son or daughter to create an aerial view drawing of his or her shoe. The shoe is to be drawn to actual size. First, have your teenager draw what he or she sees looking down on the shoe. After the sketch is completed, discuss where, why, and when an aerial view of something might be useful in daily life.

How Is Your Balance? Research points to the fact that most serious falls are related to loss of balance. While the problem is usually discussed as it relates to older adults, it is never too early to begin strengthening every family member's balance. The whole family begins by standing on one foot, without moving, for one minute. Repeat with the opposite foot. When someone can stand absolutely still on one foot for three minutes, increase the level of difficulty by doing the same exercise with your eyes closed. Repeating this simple exercise daily will help everyone in the family see an improvement in his or her balance.

Your middle schooler might enjoy reading one of the following books:

The Giver
by Lois Lowry

My Brother Sam Is Dead
by James Lincoln Collier and Christopher Collier

Across Five Aprils
by Irene Hunt

My Week at a Glance

Use this page to set goals and make journal entries.

Goals for Monday_____

_____

Journal: Pretend that you can travel back in time. Where and to what time period would you go? Who would you want to meet? What would you ask this person?

_____

_____

_____

_____

Goals for Tuesday_____

Goals for Wednesday_____

_____

Journal: You have been given a choice of being either a writer or an artist. Which would you choose? Why? What would you create?

_____

_____

_____

_____

Goals for Thursday_____

_____

Goals for Friday_____

_____

Journal: Charlie Brown, Dennis the Menace, Peter Pan, and other characters live in situations where time stands still, and they never grow up. Describe what you think it would be like to never age.

_____

_____

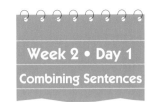

What a Combination!

Short sentences can sometimes make writing sound choppy. By combining sentences, you can help make your writing read more smoothly.

Example: My best friend loves to go horseback riding. I love to go horseback riding.
My best friend and I love to go horseback riding.

Read each pair of sentences below. Then combine the sentences into one sentence. Write the new sentence on the lines.

1. **My mom made my favorite dessert. She made pecan pie.**

_____

2. **On vacation we went swimming every day. We collected shells on the beach every day.**

_____

3. **Beethoven was a brilliant composer. He eventually lost his hearing.**

_____

4. **Charles Dickens wrote *A Tale of Two Cities*. Charles Dickens is my favorite writer.**

_____

5. **Ants are tiny creatures of great strength. Ants can lift ten times their own weight.**

_____

6. **Carmen can jump higher than anyone else on the track team. She can also jump farther than anyone on the team.**

_____

7. **One of my best friends is Matt Johnson. He is a great baseball player.**

_____

8. **My family's pet is an all-white cat. She is named Snowball.**

_____

9. **The car wash was closed yesterday. The bank was closed, too.**

_____

10. **The parade will have marching bands. The parade will have colorful floats.**

_____

Fraction Action

Solve the problems. Be sure you check the signs. Give your answers in the lowest terms.

1. $\dfrac{4}{7}$

    $+ \dfrac{6}{11}$

5. $\dfrac{6}{9}$

    $+ 1\dfrac{7}{18}$

9. $3\dfrac{7}{9}$

    $+ 4\dfrac{4}{9}$

13. $2\dfrac{3}{4}$

     $+ 3\dfrac{4}{5}$

2. $\dfrac{4}{5}$

    $- \dfrac{3}{5}$

6. $\dfrac{2}{5}$

    $- \dfrac{1}{3}$

10. $4\dfrac{1}{3}$

     $- 1\dfrac{2}{5}$

14. $4\dfrac{1}{4}$

     $- 1\dfrac{5}{6}$

3. $2 \cdot \dfrac{1}{4} =$

7. $\dfrac{2}{3} \cdot \dfrac{2}{3} =$

11. $3\dfrac{3}{4} \cdot 2 =$

15. $3\dfrac{1}{7} \cdot 1\dfrac{3}{4} =$

4. $3 \div \dfrac{1}{4} =$

8. $\dfrac{1}{2} \div \dfrac{4}{5} =$

12. $6 \div 3\dfrac{2}{3} =$

16. $1\dfrac{1}{5} \div 2\dfrac{1}{6} =$

Capitalization & Punctuation

Read each group of sentences. Circle the one sentence that shows correct capitalization and punctuation.

1. A. Jessica called, and wants to know if you *saw life as we know it.*
   B. The movie was good, but the ticket price was too high.
   C. My friends and I, go to the Movies about once a week.
   D. We pay for our movie tickets, by working on Saturday.

2. A. Ronda wondered, "where does the foil come from to make the experiment?'
   B. "The foil is always here when we start the experiment said Tommy.
   C. "Before we arrive," Emily added, "Mr. Daily sets up the lab."
   D. "I think you are right," said Audrey

3. A. A computer and monitor will cost about one thousand dollars.
   B. The desk that you ordered, will arrive next Monday.
   C. When the desk and computer are delivered, my brother, and I will help.
   D. How much should I pay for delivery.

4. A. Rachel was born on October 10 1997
   B. Rachel was born on October 10, 1997
   C. Rachel was born on October 10. 1997.
   D. Rachel was born on October 10, 1997.

5. A. Marcia asked, "Will you be going to the party with us tomorrow, Julie?"
   B. Marcia asked, Will you be going to the party with us tomorrow Julie?"
   C. Marcia asked, "Will you be going to the party with us tomorrow, Julie."
   D. Marcia asked; "Will you be going to the party with us tomorrow, Julie?"

6. A. "Stop thief! she screamed
   B. "Stop thief!" she screamed
   C. "Stop thief!" she screamed.
   D. "Stop thief," she screamed!

7. A. My friend Marcus, who is an artist displays his works at the small corner gallery downtown.
   B. Before the movie began, we had to sit through many boring commercials?
   C. My mother's job is quite demanding; however, she is on time every day.
   D. Do you know where we are, Thomas?" inquired Toshiko.

8. A. Our plane will arrive in Boston by 11 o'clock because the pilot took a shortcut.
   B. Besides Elvis Presley, who has had the most influence on rock music?
   C. My sister always asks, "When will I get my driver's license?"
   D. All the above sentences are correct.

9. A. Peter can speak English Chinese, French and Japanese.
   B. Juan enjoys playing soccer but Oscar prefers playing field hockey
   C. Have you read John steinbecks book *Travels with Charley*?
   D. All the above sentences are incorrect.

10. A. We visited Utah, Idaho, and Wyoming.
    B. We visited Utah Idaho, and Wyoming.
    C. We visited Utah, Idaho, and Wyoming
    D. We visited Utah Idaho and Wyoming.

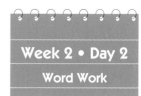

Order, Please!

Read each set of words below. Place the words in order as directed. Then compare your choices with a friend or family member to see if they agree.

1.   trot   creep   dash   amble   jog

_____   _____   _____   _____   _____

(slow → fast)

2.   tiny   bulky   infinitesimal   gargantuan   intermediate

_____   _____   _____   _____   _____

(small → large)

3.   hideous   stunning   unsightly   attractive   pleasant

_____   _____   _____   _____   _____

(ugly → beautiful)

4.   state   whisper   bark   bellow   shout

_____   _____   _____   _____   _____

(soft → loud)

5.   bland   interesting   motivating   exhilarating   mind-numbing

_____   _____   _____   _____   _____

(boring → exciting)

6.   delicate   sturdy   robust   omnipotent   sound

_____   _____   _____   _____   _____

(weak → strong)

7.   dazzling   gloomy   jet-black   shady   luminous

_____   _____   _____   _____   _____

(dark → bright)

8.   blissful   despondent   content   downcast   ecstatic

_____   _____   _____   _____   _____

(sad → happy)

Order of Operations Review

The mnemonic, **P**lease **E**xcuse **M**y **D**ear **A**unt **S**ally, is a great way to remember the order of operations in a math problem. Here's how it works:

<u>P</u>lease is for <u>p</u>arentheses.	First, calculate inside the parentheses.
<u>E</u>xcuse is for <u>e</u>xponents.	Second, find the value of terms with exponents.
<u>M</u>y <u>D</u>ear is for <u>m</u>ultiplication or <u>d</u>ivision.	Third, multiply or divide.
<u>A</u>unt <u>S</u>ally is for <u>a</u>ddition or <u>s</u>ubtraction.	Last, add or subtract.

Example: 3^2 x (4 + 3) + 6 ÷ 3

1) Work inside <u>parentheses</u> first.
2) Next, simplify any terms with <u>exponents</u>.
3) <u>Multiply</u> and <u>divide</u> from left to right.
4) <u>Add</u> and <u>subtract</u> from left to right.

3^2 x (4 + 3) + 6 ÷ 3
3^2 x 7 + 6 ÷ 3
9 x 7 + 6 ÷ 3
63 + 2
65

Evaluate each of the following expressions.

1. **(8 – 2) 2 • 2 =**

2. **(13 – 32) • 4 =**

3. **(27 ÷ 32) • 7 =**

4. **(9 + 6) ÷ 3 =**

5. **(8 – 1) • 4 + 3 =**

6. **22 • 10 ÷ 5 + 3 =**

7. **(17 – 10) – 7 =**

8. **9 + 42 – 2 =**

9. **10 – 22 • 2 =**

10. **52 + 3 • 2 =**

11. **(5 + 2) • (4 + 3) =**

12. **76 – 7 • 22 =**

13. **2 • (3 + 5) – 7 =**

14. **24 – 22 • 3 =**

15. **(62 – 3) + 5 =**

16. **6 ((9 + 5) –2 (3)) =**

17. **(8 – 1) • 4 + 3 =**

18. **4 + (22 – 3) + 5 =**

19. **2 (6 (9 +5) – 2 (3)) =**

20. **(52 – 5) • 5 ÷ 25 =**

Challenge: What combination of operations would make the following statement true?

(15 ___ 3) ___ 17 ___ 1 = 205

An Albatross Around Your Neck

Have you ever heard someone say, "It's like an albatross around my neck"? People sometimes use this phrase to describe a burden they want to overcome. The expression comes from a **ballad**, or poem, written by Samuel Taylor Coleridge in 1798, called "The Rime of the Ancient Mariner."

In the poem, a curse forces an old **mariner** to stop everyone he meets so he can tell his tale. The tale he tells is about how he and his fellow sailors became lost at sea during a terrifying storm. Their ship has been blown off course and then freezes in the icy water. Then, the sailors see an albatross, or sea bird. Soon after seeing it, the ice melts and the albatross flies with them to more peaceful waters. The sailors praise the bird as a good luck charm. However, as soon as they begin to celebrate, the mariner shoots the albatross.

Afterward, the crew experiences much hardship and misfortune. They blame their bad luck on the mariner's action. As punishment for his crime, the sailors hang the albatross around the mariner's neck. And for the rest of his life, he was forced to tell his tale to everyone he met.

Answer the following questions.

1. **An *albatross* is—**
   A. a ship.
   B. a sea bird.
   C. a sailor.
   D. a poem.

2. **According to the description of the poem, what happens first?**
   A. The mariner shoots the albatross.
   B. Sailors face a storm at sea.
   C. The mariner is forced to wear the bird.
   D. The ship is caught in the ice.

3. **Another word for *mariner* is—**
   A. bird.
   B. sea.
   C. poet.
   D. sailor.

4. **Sailors saw the albatross as ___ because ___**
   A. bad luck; they got lost.
   B. good luck; their ship was freed.
   C. dangerous; it damaged the ship.
   D. punishment; it smelled bad.

5. **Why did the mariner shoot the bird?**
   A. jealousy.
   B. hunger.
   C. fear.
   D. the answer is not given.

6. **A *ballad* is a—**
   A. sea bird.
   B. type of sailor.
   C. punishment.
   D. type of poem.

7. **In 1798,**
   A. Coleridge's poem was written.
   B. a mariner shot an albatross.
   C. the albatross was discovered.
   D. albatross-inspired clothes were popular.

8. **What was the mariner's crime?**
   A. He encountered an albatross.
   B. He got the crew lost.
   C. He shot the albatross.
   D. He wrote a bad poem.

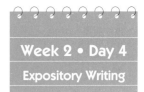
Expository or Informational Essays

Many standardized tests ask students to write an essay in response to a prompt. Students are often given a few prompts to choose from. Write some notes about each prompt below. Then use your notes to choose a prompt for an essay. Write your essay on a separate sheet of paper.

Prompt 1
Write some notes explaining why someone you care about is important to you.

_____

_____

_____

_____

_____

Prompt 2
Write some notes explaining how you have changed since you entered middle school.

_____

_____

_____

_____

_____

Prompt 3
Write some notes explaining the importance of honesty in a friendship.

_____

_____

_____

_____

_____

"Big Wind"

When several thunderstorms spiral together and grow into one giant storm, it is no longer a thunderstorm—it's a hurricane. Officially, scientists consider a storm a hurricane once its winds reach 74 mph (miles per hour). The word *hurricane* comes from the Taino Indian word *urican*, meaning "big wind." In the Atlantic Ocean, hurricanes only start in the tropics—the area five degrees north or south of the equator. If a large area of water in this part of the ocean is at least 80° F, and wind is blowing westward from Africa, conditions are just right for a hurricane. The warm, moist air of the ocean rises. As it rises, it cools, causing the water vapor to condense and form cumulonimbus clouds. As the cloud column grows larger and higher, it creates a circular pattern of wind. As the winds circle faster and faster, they twist around a calm center, called the eye. Once hurricanes hit land, they weaken because warm ocean water is no longer available to help them grow. But before they weaken, these fierce storms can cause severe damage.

Read each of the following questions and write the letter for the best answer on the line provided.

_____ 1. **For a hurricane to form in the Atlantic Ocean, the water temperature must be—**
    A. less than 80° F.   C. at least 80° F.
    B. 74 mph.   D. 5 degrees.

_____ 2. **At what wind speed do scientists classify thunderstorms as hurricanes?**
    A. 30 mph   C. 80 mph
    B. 74 mph   D. 50 mph

_____ 3. **The calm center of a hurricane is called the—**
    A. vapor.   C. eye.
    B. tropics.   D. urican.

_____ 4. **Hurricanes weaken when—**
    A. they hit land.   C. wind blows from Africa.
    B. they form cumulonimbus clouds.   D. warm, moist air rises.

Decide if the following statements are True (**T**) or False (**F**).
Write your choice on the line provided.

_____ 1.   *Hurricane* **comes from the Taino Indian word** *urican.*

_____ 2.   **The tropics is an area five degrees north and five degrees south of the equator.**

_____ 3.   **Cumulonimbus clouds cause hurricanes.**

_____ 4.   **The eye of the hurricane has the strongest winds.**

Tangrams, "The Broken Squares"

A tangram consists of a square divided into seven geometric shapes: two large triangles, one medium triangle, two small triangles, one square, and one parallelogram. These pieces can be arranged into many geometric shapes and "pictures." Tangrams are one of the oldest geometric puzzles in the world.

Here's a story often told about how tangrams came to be. About 4,000 years ago in China, a man named Tan was on his way to show the emperor his treasured tile. But the tile fell to the floor and broke into seven pieces. For the rest of his life, Tan entertained himself and his friends with his "pictures" created from these seven pieces. He first used the tile pieces to make a picture of his cat and the pagoda where he often meditated. Tan's puzzle has been passed from generation to generation and country to country. It is said that more than three hundred designs hide within the "broken square."

Directions for folding and cutting a tangram.

Step 1—Cut a four-inch by four-inch square out of heavy paper; the front of a cereal box works well.

Step 2—Draw a diagonal that divides the square into two congruent triangles. Cut along the line to separate.

Step 3—Fold one of the two congruent triangles into two smaller congruent triangles. Cut along the fold to separate.

Step 4—Take the other large triangle and fold the top point (vertice A) to the midpoint of line segment BC. Then cut along the fold to create the middle-sized triangle and a trapezoid.

Step 5—Fold the trapezoid in half as shown in the diagram so that endpoints B and C meet. Cut in half at the fold to create two trapezoids.

Step 6—Cut one trapezoid into a triangle and quadrilateral.

Step 7—Cut the other trapezoid into a square and a triangle.

Step 8—Now you should have 2 large triangles, 1 medium triangle, 2 small triangles, 1 square, and 1 parallelogram.

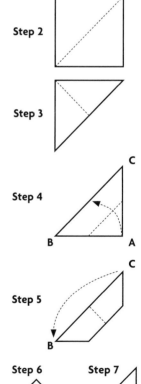

31

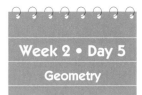

Solving Tangram Problems

Now that you have created your tangram, use the pieces to solve the following puzzles.
The number in the center of the design represents the number of tangram pieces in the puzzle.

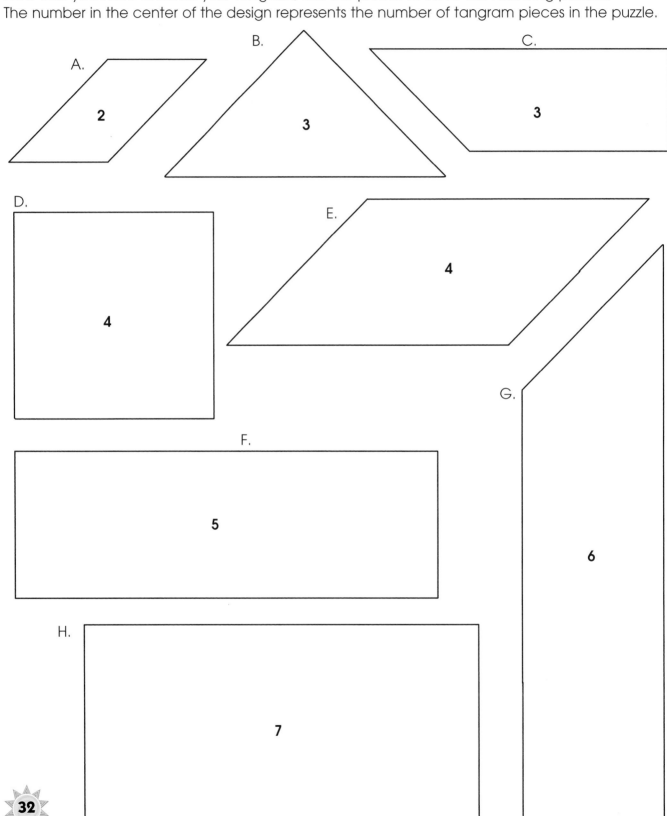

Here are the skills your middle schooler will be working on this week.

Math
- converting numbers: decimals and percents
- decimal review
- word problems

Reading
- fact vs. opinion
- reading for information

Writing
- narrative writing

Vocabulary
- figurative language
- word work: homophones
- word work: synonyms

Grammar
- gerunds

Here are some activities you and your middle schooler might enjoy:

Create a Scrapbook Help your son or daughter create a scrapbook of your family. If possible, collect pictures and copies of documents, such as birth certificates, wedding announcements, and so on from grandparents or other relatives. Be sure to have him or her label each entry with a caption.

Leave Notes Have a place in your house to leave notes either on sticky notes posted daily or on a write-on/wipe-off board. Write a positive note to a family member each day in "text message" style. Share them each evening and discuss the correct spellings of those abbreviated or shortened words.

Your middle schooler might enjoy reading one of the following books:

The Land I Lost
by Quang Nhuong Huynh

Secret, Lies, and Algebra
by Wendy Lichtman

The Battle of the Labyrinth
by Rick Riordan

 # My Week at a Glance

Use this page to set goals and make journal entries.

Goals for Monday _____

_____

Journal: Imagine you can read other people's minds. How would this talent be useful? What problems do you think might arise for others and yourself?

_____

_____

_____

_____

Goals for Tuesday _____

Goals for Wednesday _____

_____

Journal: What things in your life give you joy? Describe what a joyful day looks and feels like.

_____

_____

_____

_____

Goals for Thursday _____

_____

Goals for Friday _____

_____

Journal: If you had been with Dorothy when she finally met the Wizard, what would you have asked for? Why?

_____

_____

_____

Distinguishing Fact From Opinion

Understanding the difference between facts and opinions is essential for good readers. Statements that are facts can be proved. Opinions express a person's thoughts, beliefs, or judgments.

Read the following sentences. Circle **F** if the sentence states a fact, and **O** if it expresses an opinion.

1. **F O**   The longest and strongest bone in the human body is the femur, or thigh bone.

2. **F O**   A good athlete has broken at least one bone.

3. **F O**   Bones contain calcium.

4. **F O**   Worms have no skeletons at all.

5. **F O**   Animals that are invertebrates make better pets than vertebrates.

6. **F O**   The cranium, which protects our brain, is made up of eight bones.

7. **F O**   Most of our vital organs are protected by bones.

8. **F O**   Skeletons are very scary.

9. **F O**   Antlers are made entirely of bone.

10. **F O**   Human skeletons are more interesting than animal skeletons.

Write two more facts about bones and two more opinions.

Fact 1: _____

Fact 2: _____

Opinion 1: _____

Opinion 2: _____

Juggling Gerunds

 *A **gerund** is a verb that ends in –ing and acts as a **noun** in a sentence. A gerund can act as a subject, direct object, subject complement (predicate nominative), or object of a preposition. In the following sentences, the gerund is underlined, and the gerund's function is given in the parentheses.*

Examples:

Swimming in this lake is my favorite pastime. (subject)

Jessica enjoys swimming. (direct object)

Brian's most recent exercise program is swimming. (subject complement or predicate nominative)

The instructor taught us the skills of swimming. (object of preposition)

A **gerund phrase** includes the gerund, its modifiers, and the words that complete the idea begun by the gerund. In the following sentence, the simple gerund is in bold; the gerund phrase is underlined.

Swimming on our vacation was so much fun for the entire family.

Underline each gerund phrase once. Underline the gerund twice. Then identify whether the gerund in each sentence functions as a subject (**S**), predicate nominative (**PN**), direct object (**DO**), or object of a preposition (**OP**).

_____ 1. **Studying art also taught Gerald about art history.**

_____ 2. **Today was my first attempt at playing kickball.**

_____ 3. **Entering the contest was my mother's idea.**

_____ 4. **Ava's next class is dancing.**

_____ 5. **Reporting the news is Jessica's dream job.**

_____ 6. **Mrs. Palmer was given an award for volunteering her time.**

_____ 7. **Being the secretary of the art club is such a big responsibility.**

_____ 8. **Pressing the wrong button on this computer can be quite dangerous.**

_____ 9. **Alberto prefers taking photos of landscapes.**

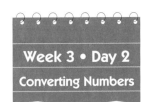
Decimals & Percents

Any decimal can be converted to a percent by simply moving the decimal two places to the right and adding a percent sign. When a decimal contains thousandths or smaller percents, still move the decimal two places to the right. The percent will contain a decimal point.

Examples:

Convert .23 to %   *Convert* .943 to %

.23 = 23%   .943 = 94.3%

To convert percents to decimals, move the decimal point two places to the left, and remove the percentage sign.

Examples:

Convert 45%   *Convert* 102%

45.   102.

Convert the decimals to percents, and the percents to decimals.

1. **.6** _____

2. **.43** _____

3. **91.6%** _____

4. **.05** _____

5. **3.11** _____

6. **6%** _____

7. **8.955** _____

8. **.731** _____

9. **.82** _____

10. **56.85%** _____

11. **119%** _____

12. **105%** _____

13. **.5** _____

14. **1.05** _____

15. **101.75** _____

16. **.695** _____

17. **1.943** _____

18. **2%** _____

19. **.013** _____

20. **41.46** _____

21. **.008** _____

22. **2.321** _____

23. **98.2%** _____

24. **.15** _____

25. **33.5%** _____

26. **223.23** _____

27. **3.4** _____

28. **.997** _____

29. **.14** _____

30. **9.775** _____

Figurative Language

Review the following definitions of various kinds of figurative language.

Similes *Comparisons using connecting words, such as* like, as, *or* seems.
Example: A smile like a sunbeam brightened her face.

Metaphors *are comparisons that use no connecting words.*
Example: The clouds are fluffy pillows.

Personification *appears frequently in poetry as well as prose.*
Personification is giving human characteristics to things that are not human.
Example: The storm knocked on our windows.

Hyperbole *is an obvious exaggeration used to emphasize a point or add excitement and/or humor to a story.*
Example: The walk from the car to the doctor's office took forever with my broken toe.

Read each of the following statements. Identify which of the four figurative language terms it represents. Write the answer in the blank provided.

_____ 1. **The leaves danced across the yard.**

_____ 2. **The old, silent house remembered the happy days when laughing children filled its rooms.**

_____ 3. **I am so hungry I could eat a horse.**

_____ 4. **The pet dog is another child in the family.**

_____ 5. **Jordan can be as quiet as a mouse sometimes.**

_____ 6. **Madison's bedroom was a pig's sty before she cleaned it.**

_____ 7. **Vincent is as sharp as a tack.**

_____ 8. **Yvonne bent close to Margi's ear and whispered, "Be careful, the walls have ears."**

_____ 9. **If I've told you once, I've told you a million times to close the door.**

_____ 10. **The students felt that the essay assignment was a piece of cake.**

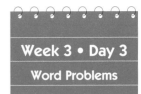

. . . And the Beat Goes On

In an adult human, the heart is only about the size of an average fist and weighs about nine ounces. This amazing muscle beats, without stopping, from before birth until death. Humans, on average, can expect more than 75 years of service from this four-chambered miracle. During its life, the heart will pump millions of quarts of blood through the body. An average rate for a typical 13-year-old is about 80 or 85 beats per minute. During exercise, the number of beats per minute can double.

Your task now is to estimate how hard your heart is working for you every minute, hour, and day of your life. Use a calculator and find out.

1. **If a normal heart beats around 80 beats per minute,**

    A. how many beats occur in an hour?   _____

    B. how many beats in a 24-hour day?   _____

    C. how many beats in a year?   _____

2. **If the heart continues to beat at 80 beats per minute for 75 years, what is the total number of beats?**

    _____

3. **If the average person has a normal heart beat of 80 beats per minute and the heart pumps 5 quarts per minute,**

    A. how much blood would the heart pump in a 24-hour day? _____

    B. how much in a year? _____

4. **A marathon runner's heart can pump 30 quarts of blood per minute. Based on this statistic, how much blood would be pumped in a race that lasted 2 hours, 15 minutes, and 30 seconds?**

    _____

5. **Find a partner and a watch with a second hand. Take turns recording each other's pulse for 30 seconds. Measure pulse by placing your fore and middle fingers together on the underside of your partner's wrist; make sure you can feel the pulse beat. Count the beats in 30 seconds; then multiply by 2. Once you each have your pulse rate or heart beat, calculate the following:**

    A. How many times does your heart beat in an hour? _____

    B. How many times in a year? _____

Narrative Writing

Respond to one of the essay prompts below. Limit yourself to 60 minutes for completing the essay. Use the space provided to make notes, record single words, phrases, clauses, or even entire sentences for each prompt. Then decide which prompt to use to write your essay. Write your essay on another sheet of paper.

1. **Eleanor Roosevelt once said, "You must do the thing you think you cannot do." Write a narrative about a time you did something you thought you could not do. Be sure to include specific details so that a reader can follow your essay.**

_____

_____

_____

_____

_____

2. **Think of your very best day ever at school. What happened that made this day stand out in your memory? Write an essay that tells about what happened.**

_____

_____

_____

_____

_____

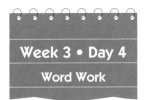

Spell Check!

Spell check on a computer is a great tool for checking your spelling, but it doesn't mean you don't have to read your writing carefully! It can sometimes miss mistakes. Some words in English sound the same, but are spelled differently and mean different things. These are called **homophones**. Spell check won't catch these kinds of errors. Read the sentences below carefully. Each one has a word that is wrong. Circle the word, and then write the correct word that should replace it on the blank line.

_____ 1. Their are lots of excellent teachers in my school.

_____ 2. Allison lost control of the horse when she dropped the reigns.

_____ 3. The principle spoke at the assembly.

_____ 4. Alonzo is known for telling wild tails.

_____ 5. I wander if I will be able to go swimming today.

_____ 6. Theirs never enough time in the day to have fun.

_____ 7. Jose likes vanilla ice cream more then chocolate.

_____ 8. Miranda thought Alex had eaten far to many hot dogs.

_____ 9. Nathan spent hours pouring over his new comic books.

_____ 10. The picnic had to be cancelled because of bad whether.

_____ 11. Its supposed to be sunny for the rest of the week.

_____ 12. Everyone in my swim class past the water safety test.

_____ 13. Amanda one the summer reading challenge at the library.

_____ 14. The weight for the train was longer than we expected.

_____ 15. Josh's favorite food is stake.

_____ 16. Audrey ran down the stares when she heard the doorbell ring.

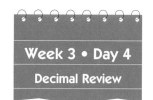
Decimal Operations

To add or subtract with decimals, *remember to line up the decimal points. Use zeros as place holders so that the number of digits to the right of the decimal point remain consistent. Adding zeros to the right of the final digit in a decimal does not affect its value.*

Line up the decimal points properly; add zeros if necessary and solve.

1. **237.895 + 30.25 =**

2. **7.4036 + 13.765 + .1437 =**

3. **7.4036 − .1437 =**

4. **.3862 + 1.45 + 5.097 =**

5. **897.0352 − 46.0231 =**

6. **2.431 + 9.56 + 4.675 =**

To multiply with decimals, *first multiply as usual, then count the number of places to the right of the decimal point in each of the factors. Count that number of places, starting at the right-most digit in the product, and place the decimal point there. If there are not enough digits, add zeros on the left of the product before placing the decimal point.*

To divide with decimals, *place a decimal point in the quotient directly above the one in the dividend. Use zero as a place holder as needed. When dividing a decimal by a decimal, first count the number of digits to the right of the decimal point in the divisor. Move the point in both the dividend and the divisor that number of places to the right, adding zeros as place holders.*

Solve the following.

7.   1.80
    x 3.29

8. 19$\overline{)64.6}$

9.   0.02
    x 0.03

10. 4$\overline{)26.88}$

11.   3.7
    x 4.5

12. 0.16$\overline{)24.}$

13.   .03
    x .2

14. 0.4$\overline{)972.5}$

Out and Over

Play the game of Out and Over—and boost your vocabulary! Find a word in Box 1 that is *not* a synonym of the other three words. Move that word to Box 2 (where it will be a **synonym**) by writing it on the blank line. Continue until you reach Box 12. Then complete the sentence in that box.

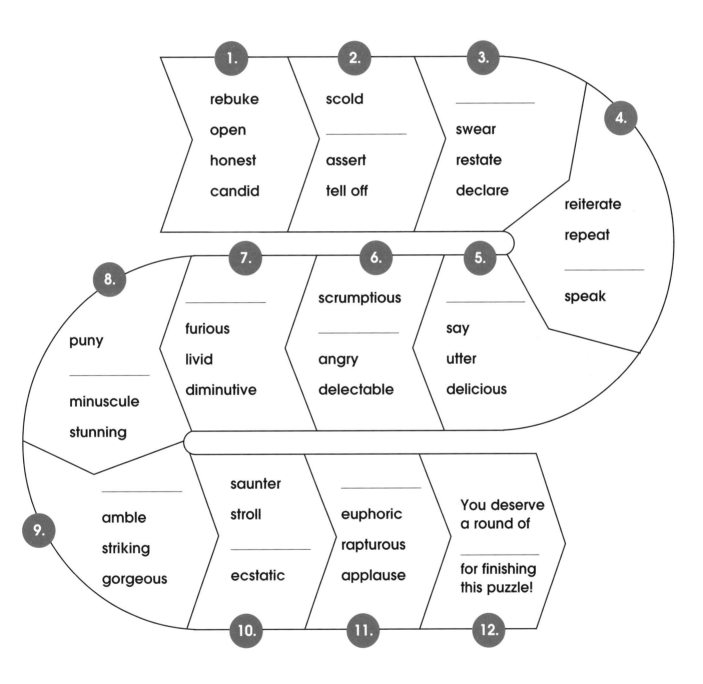

1.
rebuke
open
honest
candid

2.
scold
_____
assert
tell off

3.
_____
swear
restate
declare

4.
reiterate
repeat
_____
speak

5.
_____
say
utter
delicious

6.
scrumptious
_____
angry
delectable

7.
_____
furious
livid
diminutive

8.
puny
_____
minuscule
stunning

9.
_____
amble
striking
gorgeous

10.
saunter
stroll
_____
ecstatic

11.
_____
euphoric
rapturous
applause

12.
You deserve a round of
_____
for finishing this puzzle!

43

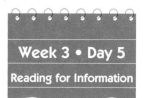
Japan's Latest Literary Craze: Novels Written on Cell Phones

When was the last time you wrote a novel? If you are a teenager in Japan, you might be writing one now on your cell phone! Cell phone novels started relatively recently. The practice began in the year 2000 but only became popular in 2005. Most cell phone novelists are young women going to school or working part-time. Whenever they have a free moment before class or work, they type out a line of the story and send it out as a text message. Readers receive the new lines directly on their phones. Some writers also post their stories on Web sites.

For most of these aspiring novelists, there is no reward but the joy of self-expression. However, some of the most popular cell phone novels have been published as actual books. A few of these authors have become famous and made a great deal of money from their work. Cell phone novels have become such a lucrative, or profitable, endeavor that some traditional novelists have started writing them, too.

Although cell phone novels were initially dismissed by critics as trivial, they are slowly gaining more support. They are a very popular genre for young people, many of whom do not normally read traditional novels. Because of their growing popularity, they are beginning to get more respect and may one day be considered a genre, or category, of literature in their own right.

Answer the following questions.

1. **Cell phone novels are—**
   A. stories about cell phones.
   B. stories sent as text messages.
   C. an example of traditional literary genre.
   D. not very popular in Japan.

2. **What happened first?**
   A. Established authors text stories.
   B. Cell phone novels become popular.
   C. Cell phone novels are published as books.
   D. Teenagers tell stories through texts.

3. **Cell phone novels are usually written by—**
   A. people who read traditional novels.
   B. publishing companies.
   C. very old men.
   D. young women.

4. **A genre is—**
   A. a type of cell phone novel.
   B. an author.
   C. a Japanese fad.
   D. a category.

5. **If an endeavor is lucrative, it means that it—**
   A. will make lots of money.
   B. may not succeed.
   C. will not be published.
   D. will become popular in Japan.

6. **Cell phone novels are popular because they—**
   A. are easy to read and relate to.
   B. make money.
   C. have always had a following in Japan.
   D. are an established genre.

Here are the skills your middle schooler will be working on this week.

Math
- fraction word problems
- geometry
- probability: tree diagrams
- problem solving

Reading
- reading comprehension
- summarizing

Writing
- persuasive writing

Vocabulary
- spelling
- Greek roots

Grammar
- infinitives

Here is an activity you and your middle schooler might enjoy:

Virtual Field Trip Everyone loves a field trip, and now with the help of the web, you and your child can explore many exciting places both on earth and beyond. NASA offers an interactive visit to the Jet Propulsion Laboratory Museum, Mission Control, the Robot Lab, and Sun Zone (http://virtualfieldtrip.jpl.nasa.gov). National Geographic offers a number of interactive games and animations that take place in six rooms of the Expedition Hall. Find the adventure at www.nationalgeographic.com/resources. The British Museum has an exciting, interactive site to learn about the secrets of ancient Egypt. The site explores the science of mummification, crafts, and hieroglyphics. Their site is located at www.ancientegypt.co.uk. Should you wish to explore closer to home, try www.history.org/visit/tourthetown to find a comprehensive tour of Colonial Williamsburg, Virginia. Many other museums, cities, and historical sites also offer virtual field trips. Note: Be sure to preview each Web site before your child visits it to verify that the site is still active and at an appropriate level.

Your middle schooler might enjoy reading one of the following books:

The Headless Cupid
by Zilpha Keatley Snyder

The Pushcart War
by Jean Merrill

The Voyages of Doctor Dolittle
by Hugh Lofting

My Week at a Glance

Use this page to set goals and make journal entries.

Goals for Monday_____

_____

Journal: The winning prize in a local raffle is the chance to have a sky writer write one sentence in the sky. You win! What will you have written? Why?

_____

_____

_____

_____

Goals for Tuesday_____

_____

Goals for Wednesday_____

_____

Journal: What is your personal definition of success?

_____

_____

_____

_____

Goals for Thursday_____

_____

Goals for Friday_____

_____

Journal: Think about and then explain what you consider to be the difference between courage and recklessness.

_____

_____

_____

_____

Spelling

Read the directions carefully. Be sure to know if you are looking for the correctly or incorrectly spelled word. When you are not sure of an answer, look at each choice and say the word to yourself. Then write in the answer that seems the best.

Find the word that is spelled *correctly* and best completes the sentence.

1. The _____ will be held next month on Tuesday.
   A. alection   B. election   C. eletion   D. elektion

2. Did I _____ we will have a birthday party this Sunday?
   A. menstion   B. mention   C. mension   D. menshun

3. Be _____ on your drive home tonight.
   A. caustious   B. caucious   C. cautus   D. cautious

4. The sun is a source of extremely cheap _____.
   A. inergy   B. energy   C. enirgy   D. energie

5. I have never visited a _____ country.
   A. foreign   B. forein   C. forin   D. foriegn

Choose the phrase in which the underlined word is not spelled correctly.

6. A. an encredible sight
   B. a predictable conclusion
   C. long delay at the airport
   D. very useful conference

7. A. a nutritious lunch
   B. blinking warning sign
   C. to remain fearless
   D. earned a free tickit

8. A. gather together tonight
   B. become too crowded
   C. a very late departure
   D. narrow hazerdous road

9. A. worthless pile of junk
   B. smooth, colorful serface
   C. tuned musical instruments
   D. accelerate around the curve

10. A. very relaible automobile
    B. a difficult obstacle
    C. incorrect test answer
    D. much enjoyment tonight

11. A. notise something
    B. rarely visit the museum
    C. an important discovery
    D. such an easy solution

12. A. arrest a criminal
    B. always a polite person
    C. cannot locate the lock
    D. work hard all weak

Functional Fractions

Solve the following problems. Show your work.

1. Crystal has 20 pets: $\frac{2}{5}$ are rabbits, $\frac{1}{2}$ are fish and $\frac{1}{10}$ are dogs. How many of each animal does she have?

2. Colin has 36 polished rocks. Of the rocks, $\frac{1}{4}$ will be used in a science experiment and $\frac{4}{9}$ will be given to his friend Tony. How many rocks will he still have?

3. June has $40.00 in her bank account. $\frac{1}{4}$ of the money must remain in the bank and $\frac{1}{2}$ of the remaining amount will be donated to her favorite charity. How much will June donate?

4. Tim caught a fish that weighed $4\frac{1}{6}$ pounds. Then he caught another that weighed $6\frac{5}{8}$ pounds. How much more did the second fish weigh?

5. In the warehouse there is a stack of 7 crates. Each crate is $10\frac{2}{3}$ inches high. How many inches high is the stack of crates?

6. Samantha has $3\frac{1}{4}$ bags of peanuts. Each bag holds $4\frac{1}{2}$ pounds. How many pounds of peanuts does Samantha have?

7. Corey spent $6\frac{1}{2}$ hours at the park on Saturday and $7\frac{3}{4}$ hours on Sunday. How many hours did Corey spend in all?

8. When the bakery closed, Marcia noted that she had $2\frac{1}{4}$ peach pies and $1\frac{1}{2}$ apple pies left. How much more peach pie than apple pie was left?

Greek Roots

Many English words have Greek roots. Some examples are given in the chart below.

Greek Root	Meaning	Example
aero	air	aerate: expose to air or allow circulating air to reach or penetrate aerobics: system of exercises designed to increase respiration and heart rate
belli	war	rebellion: uprising belligerent: aggressive or warlike
pan	all	panorama: unlimited view panacea: a cure for all problems
chronos	time	chronic: lasting a long time synchronize: to happen at the same time

Use the chart to play Tic-Tac-Toe. Read each word. Then draw a line through three words in the box that are synonyms for that word. Your line can be vertical, horizontal, or diagonal.

panacea

cure-all	answer	solution
happiness	anger	ocean
physics	mix	air

synchronize

outdated	harmonious	disorderly
heavy	coincide	nonstop
wildly	coordinate	ancient

belligerent

pugnacious	loud	melodious
autonomy	aggressive	kind
coincide	chaos	combative

aerate

listen	angry	expose
yell	ventilate	forces
freshen	mix	rebellion

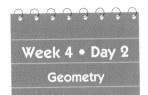

Geometry Jumble

Where is the world's oldest castle found?

To find out, unscramble each geometry word. Write the correctly spelled word in the spaces provided. The boxed letters from top to bottom reveal the location.

1. **NESTMEG** ___ ___ ⬜ ___ ___ ___ ___

2. **NECO** ___ ___ ⬜ ___

3. **ELMOVU** ___ ___ ___ ⬜ ___ ___

4. **CRINAPPLERUDE** ___ ___ ___ ___ ___ ___ ⬜ ___ ___ ___ ___ ___ ___

5. **AYR** ___ ___ ⬜

6. **GLEAN** ___ ⬜ ___ ___ ___

7. **YAMDRIP** ___ ⬜ ___ ___ ___ ___ ___

8. **PESHER** ___ ___ ___ ⬜ ___ ___

9. **MIRPS** ___ ___ ⬜ ___ ___

10. **REXVET** ___ ___ ___ ⬜ ___ ___

11. **PINTO** ___ ___ ___ ⬜ ___

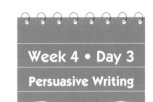

Persuasive Prompt

Writing Situation:
Girls and boys often enjoy playing the same sports and play with equal skill. Some people believe that girls and boys should be able to play on the same team. What is your opinion on this issue?

Directions for Writing:
Write a letter to the school board stating your opinion and supporting it with convincing reasons.

_____ (Date)

_____ (Salutation)

_____

_____

_____

_____

_____

_____

_____

_____

_____

_____

_____ (Complimentary Close)

_____ (Signature)

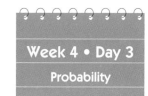
Clothes Combos

How many combinations can you make with your favorite clothes? A tree diagram can show you. For example, Doug has one baseball cap, three shirts, and two pairs of pants. If he chooses one hat, one shirt and one pair of pants for each outfit, how many outfits can he make?

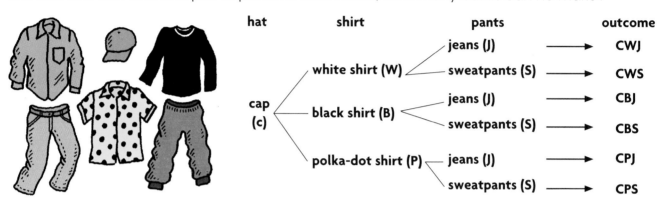

1. **How many of Doug's outfits include a baseball cap?** _____

2. **How many outfits include a white shirt?** _____

3. **How many outfits include jeans?** _____

Fill in this tree diagram to find out which different outfits Stella can make with her clothes. She can pick one shirt, one skirt, and one pair of shoes for each outfit. Here's what she's got: polka-dot shirt, striped shirt, long skirt, short skirt, sneakers, and sandals.

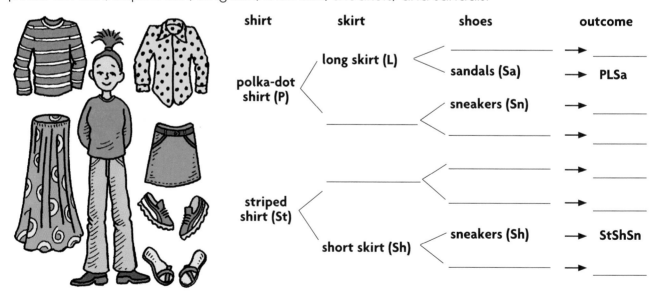

4. **How many of Stella's outfits include a striped shirt?** _____

5. **How many outfits include a long skirt?** _____

6. **How many outfits include sneakers?** _____

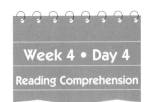
Tsunami Warning

A **tsunami** is an unusually massive wave. These huge waves can be caused by an earthquake, a volcanic eruption, a landslide, or a meteorite impact. Tsunamis occur most frequently in the Pacific Ocean, but they can appear in any body of water, even in lakes.

The most common cause of a tsunami is an undersea earthquake. During an undersea earthquake, tectonic plates shift and the sea floor rapidly changes shape. These changes can cause water to be shifted up quickly, resulting in a tsunami.

The word *tsunami* comes from Japanese, and it means "harbor wave." Japanese fishermen called tsunamis harbor waves because they often have little effect on the open ocean, but devastate coastal villages and harbors. So, a fisherman might have had a peaceful day at sea and come home to discover his village has been destroyed by a tsunami.

Tsunamis used to be known as "tidal waves" but this is a **misnomer**. Geologists and oceanographers consider "tidal wave" an inappropriate name for a tsunami because tidal waves are caused by the gravitational pull of the moon. In contrast, tsunamis are normally caused by seismic activity such as undersea earthquakes. For this reason, scientists prefer the term **seismic sea waves**. Although, at high tide, when the moon's gravitational pull on the ocean is the strongest and the ocean level is the highest, tsunamis are much more destructive.

Answer the following questions.

1. **Tsunami is a Japanese word meaning—**
   A. tidal wave.
   B. harbor wave.
   C. gravitational pull.
   D. misnomer.

2. **During an undersea earthquake, first—**
   A. tectonic plates shift.
   B. the tsunami strikes the shore.
   C. water rapidly rises.
   D. the sea floor is pushed up.

3. **Tsunamis are most dangerous—**
   A. on peaceful days.
   B. at low tide.
   C. at high tide.
   D. during a drought.

4. **Seismic sea waves are also known as—**
   A. tornadoes.
   B. tsunamis.
   C. misnomers.
   D. hurricanes.

5. **A misnomer is—**
   A. a female gnome.
   B. a type of tsunami.
   C. a type of tidal wave.
   D. an inappropriate name.

6. **The moon's gravitational pull causes—**
   A. tsunamis.
   B. tidal waves.
   C. undersea earthquakes.
   D. seismic sea waves.

7. **Why is a tsunami more harmful at high tide?**
   A. The water level is already high.
   B. The fishermen are at sea.
   C. Oceanographers have lunch then.
   D. Everyone is at the beach.

8. **Tsunamis only occur—**
   A. near coastal villages.
   B. near bodies of water, excluding lakes.
   C. in the Pacific ocean.
   D. in bodies of water, including lakes.

Identifying Infinitives and Infinitive Phrases

 *An **infinitive** is a verb form consisting of the word* to *plus a verb, for example: "to read," "to know," and "to pretend." An infinitive can function as a noun, adjective, or adverb. The* **simple infinitive** *is the word* to *plus the verb. The **infinitive phrase** is the infinitive, its modifiers, plus its complements.*

Tip: *To decide whether a phrase is an infinitive phrase or a prepositional phrase, look at the word after* to. *If the word is a verb, the phrase is an infinitive. If the word is a noun, pronoun, or modifier, the phrase is a prepositional phrase.*

Does Marcia want <u>to write the presidential report</u>? (infinitive phrase)
The president spoke <u>to the reporters</u> after the assembly program. (prepositional phrase)

Underline the infinitive phrase in each sentence.

1. Our class is planning to exhibit our artwork in the cafeteria.

2. Do you want to paint the background wall on Saturday?

3. Our family went to see the Fourth of July parade.

4. We left the train station early to see all the floats in the parade.

5. Please pay the admission fee to enter the amusement park.

6. Who wants to run to the grocery store for cheese and crackers?

7. Jonah was pleased to hear the news this morning.

8. My mother was quite happy to read my essay.

9. The only way to have a friend is to be one.

10. To cook breakfast for our family, you will need a much larger skillet.

11. To reach the Italian restaurant, turn right at the next street.

12. Mother's suggestion was to leave by 4:00 P.M.

13. It was Tony's idea to take a taxi instead of the train.

14. To score the most points is the object of the game.

Car for Rent

Here's your chance to see the U.S.A.— without leaving your home!

The following car rental plans are from Take Off Rent-a-Car.

Plan A	Plan B	Plan C
$32.95 per day	$27.95 per day	$45 per day
500 free miles	no free miles	1,500 free miles
then $0.20 a mile	$0.25 a mile	then $0.30 a mile

1. Choose a North American destination you'd like to visit. How about the Statue of Liberty, Big Bend National Park, Monument Valley, or the Everglades? Plot a route to the spot you pick. Map out and record the route and estimate the driving distance.

_____

_____

_____

2. Figure out how long the entire round-trip would take. Remember: You can't drive all day long, and you need to sleep, eat, get gas, and spend some time at the place you're visiting. And don't forget those speed limits!

_____

_____

_____

3. Using each plan, determine the cost of the car rental for your entire round-trip. Which plan makes the most sense for you? Why?

_____

_____

_____

55

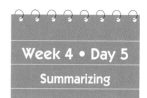

Pedal Power

On Monday mornings, city streets are jammed with cars and buses filled with commuters. Take a closer look, and you might see plenty of people pedaling their way to work or school. The number of bike commuters has more than tripled over the past two decades. Worldwide, three times more bikes are built than cars.

Why do so many Americans like to ride bikes? Biking is a fun way to get outdoors and to exercise. More people are discovering that on a bike, they can get in shape and get where they need to go at the same time. In fact, nearly five million Americans commute to work on bicycles.

Two major bike-to-work cities are Tucson, Arizona, and San Diego, California. In these areas, warm weather makes year-round biking possible. Surprisingly, rainy Seattle, Washington, and chilly Minneapolis, Minnesota, both have high rates of bicycle commuters.

Cities are racing to make the ride easier. More bike commuters mean fewer cars. Fewer cars mean less of a need for new roads. Creating bike paths or "Bikes Only" lanes on streets is far less expensive than building roads.

Officials in Portland, Oregon, came up with a unique idea. They wanted to encourage people to bike around town instead of driving. So the city rounded up used bikes—ones that people would have just thrown away. They repaired them and painted them yellow. Then they put the yellow bikes around the city and spread the word that they were free for anyone to use. When borrowers reach their destination, they just leave the bike for someone else. People are pedaling the yellow bikes all over Portland. The public bike fleet is growing as more people donate old bikes. Will your town be next? About 50 cities have asked Portland how to start their own public pedal-power program!

All of these healthy bikers help create a healthier environment. When it comes to planet-friendly modes of transportation, you can't beat a bike. Unlike cars, bikes burn no fossil fuels and create no air pollution. In addition, computer-aided design and new technologies have helped create a new breed of bicycles that make riding safer, easier, and a lot more fun.

Write one paragraph summarizing what you read in "Pedal Power."

_____

_____

_____

_____

_____

_____

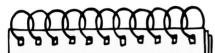

Here are the skills your middle schooler will be working on this week.

Math
- variables
- estimation
- basic operations review
- algebra

Reading
- following directions
- reading comprehension

Writing
- descriptive writing

Vocabulary
- portmanteau

Grammar
- parts of speech

Here are some activities that you and your middle schooler might enjoy:

Drop by a Community Service Center Ask your middle schooler to join some friends in making cool posters, cards, or even a snack for the employees of a fire station or other service station. When you deliver the items or food with the children, you might arrange a tour to see first-hand what the employees' jobs involve.

Dance! Dance! Dance! Have your child try this activity alone (with no one watching!) or with a friend or two. Find a television channel or go to the library to check out an instructional video on salsa or ballroom dancing, hip hop, or whatever dance style your child wants to try. Then encourage him or her to start learning each step. Soon, your child will be bustin' out some amazing moves!

Your middle schooler might enjoy reading one of the following books:

Catherine, Called Birdy
by Karen Cushman

Johnny Tremain
by Esther Forbes

Zen and the Art of Faking It
by Jordan Sonnenblick

My Week at a Glance

Use this page to set goals and make journal entries.

Goals for Monday_____

_____

Journal: By now you have studied many explorers from history. With whom would you have chosen to travel? Why?

_____

_____

_____

_____

Goals for Tuesday_____

_____

Goals for Wednesday_____

_____

Journal: You are probably familiar with poems called *haiku*. The poem has three lines: the first line has five syllables; the second has seven; the third has five. Use this pattern to create a haiku about yourself.

_____

_____

_____

_____

Goals for Thursday_____

_____

Goals for Friday_____

_____

Journal: Flying cars have long been a dream concept of inventors. What might be some advantages and disadvantages of such a vehicle?

_____

_____

_____

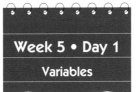
Evaluating Variable Expressions

*In math, a **variable** is a letter used to represent one or more numbers in a mathematical expression.*

Example: Evaluate $\dfrac{22}{y}$ when y = 2

$$\dfrac{22}{2} = 11$$

Evaluate each expression when y = 2.

1. **8y**

2. $\dfrac{\mathbf{10}}{\mathbf{y}}$

3. **y + 3**

4. **14 – y**

Evaluate each expression when y = 5.

5. **2y – 3**

6. **y + y + 8**

7. **19 – y + 4**

8. **9 – y + 3 – 1**

The perimeter of a square is equal to 4s where s equals the length of one side.

9. **What is the perimeter of a square where s is equal to 7 feet?** _____

10. **Find the perimeter of a square where s = 123 feet.** _____

11. **James knows the perimeter of a square is 1,023 feet. He stated that one side of the square is an even whole number. Is this answer correct? Why or why not?**

_____

_____

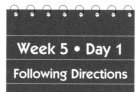

Comparing Family Recipes

These one-dish meals are easy to prepare. Add a salad, bread, beverage, and dessert, and dinner is served! With permission, you can be chef for a day and prepare dinner for the family at least twice this summer. After each meal, have each family member evaluate the hot dish. Allow the members of your family to vote to decide if the dish should be added to the family's favorites. Things to consider are as follows: taste, cost per serving, ease of preparation, and possible leftovers.

Read the recipe below. Then answer the questions.

Corn Chip Casserole

2 $15\frac{1}{2}$ oz cans chili with beans

2 $15\frac{1}{2}$ oz cans chili without beans

1 13 oz pkg. corn chips

3 cups sharp cheddar cheese, shredded

2 cups tomato sauce

3 cups enchilada sauce

2 tablespoons onion, chopped

1 $4\frac{1}{2}$ oz can olives (optional), chopped

1 4 oz can green chilies, chopped

2 cups sour cream

Preheat oven to 350°.

Reserve 1 cup corn chips, 1 cup grated cheese, and all the sour cream. Place remaining ingredients in a 4-quart casserole. Mix well and bake 30 minutes. Spread sour cream on top and garnish with remaining corn chips and grated cheese. Bake for 5 minutes longer. Serves 12.

1. What is the total baking time for this recipe? _____

2. What item is optional? _____

3. What is the total amount of chili needed for the recipe? _____

4. Elena's family of five has invited four neighbors over to share this casserole.

   Will they have enough to serve everyone? _____

5. What ingredients are used as garnish for the casserole? _____

6. What size dish is required for this recipe? _____

Show, Don't Tell

When you show, rather than tell, in your writing, you help readers create pictures in their minds. Review the examples to see the difference.

Examples:

Telling	**Showing**
Jill was happy.	Jill skipped down the hall, clapping her hands and smiling at everyone.
The puppy was scared.	Shivering and whimpering, the puppy cowered behind the couch during the storm.

Rewrite the following sentences so that you are showing, rather than telling.

1. **My room was a mess.**

_____

_____

2. **Summer camp was fun.**

_____

_____

3. **Making cupcakes left a big mess in the kitchen.**

_____

_____

4. **The soccer game was bad.**

_____

_____

5. **The dinner was good.**

_____

_____

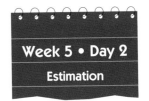
Estimation: Using Rounding

Solve the problems below, using only estimation. Using a calculator, pencil, or paper is not allowed. Round your answers to the nearest dollar.

Shop at Mac's Markdown
—where all prices include sales tax!

Jeans

Boot Cut	$39.99
Flares	$48.62
Skinny	$72.95

Shoes

Sneakers	$66.78
Boots	$99.99
Flip Flops	$24.79

Belts

Brown	$12.50
Black	$12.50

Tops

T-shirt	$13.59
Sweater	$38.79
Hoodie	$19.95

1. You have earned $150 by doing small chores around the neighborhood. Mom takes you to Mac's to shop. Use estimation to find if you have enough money to purchase a pair of boots and two pairs of flip flops. What is your estimate of the cost of the three pairs of shoes?

2. Mom gives you permission to buy one complete outfit (a pair of jeans, a top, a belt, and shoes). Your budget is $175. Find at least two different outfits within the budget.

3. Mom discovers she has only $150 in her wallet. Which items would you return or change to stay within her budget?

4. How much money would you need to buy two hoodies, three t-shirts, and one sweater?

5. Everyone in your group decides to buy the same belt. There are 6 people interested in buying belts. Will $78 be enough money to buy all 6 belts?

6. When estimating costs, one can round up or down. If you round more items down than up, will the total cost be less than or greater than your estimate? Why do you think so?

Blends

 *When parts of two words are combined, the new word that is formed is called a **blend**, or a **portmanteau**. Examples of some blends are given in the chart below.*

Word One	Word Two	Blend
smoke	fog	smog
emotion	icon	emoticon
breakfast	lunch	brunch
chuckle	snort	chortle
flout	vaunt	flaunt

Write the blend formed from each pair of words below.

1. **motor and hotel** _____

2. **situation and comedy** _____

3. **information and commercial** _____

4. **walk and marathon** _____

5. **splash and spatter** _____

Write the best blend from the chart above to complete each sentence.

6. **Alden ended his text message with a funny** _____.

7. **On weekends,** _____ **is served in the restaurant after 11am.**

8. **Alissa likes to** _____ **her diving skills.**

9. **The fire added to the layer of** _____ **over the city.**

10. **The audience began to** _____ **when the comedian told the joke.**

63

Identifying Parts of Speech

Identify the parts of speech in italics by labeling it **n.** (noun*), **pro.** (pronoun), **v.** (verb), **adj.** (adjective), **adv.** (adverb), **prep.** (preposition), **conj.** (conjunction), and **interj.** (interjection).

_____ 1. *Oh*, I left my purse and cell phone on the seat in my aunt's car.

_____ 2. *During* the party, our dog had to stay outside the house.

_____ 3. Old Faithful geyser *erupts* almost hourly.

_____ 4. The race car drove *extremely* fast.

_____ 5. *Neither* Sonja *nor* Isabelle wants to go swimming.

_____ 6. Joe and Maria usually play softball *with* Terry and Thomas.

_____ 7. *Who* told you about our trip to Spain?

_____ 8. Molly vacuumed the carpets, *and* I cleaned the windows.

_____ 9. *Ouch!* I did not know the edge of the board was so sharp.

_____ 10. Yesterday we *walked* through the park on the way home.

_____ 11. You must make a decision *before* six o'clock.

_____ 12. *They* mow lawns during the summer to earn extra money.

_____ 13. Which of the two movies did you like *better*?

_____ 14. The *oldest* clock in the world is in England.

_____ 15. My little brother *went* to play softball in the park.

_____ 16. The red brick house on the corner is *ours*.

Practice Makes Perfect

Solve the problems. Pay attention to the signs. You can use a calculator.

1. 126
    x   6

6. 7785 ÷ 45 =

11. 11,925 ÷ 225 =

2. 2,972
    - 984

7. 39,995
    + 12,699

12. 507
     x 109

3. 92,475
    - 76,097

8. 926
    x 27

13. 52,009
     - 21,950

9. 5280 ÷ 120 =

14. 108,462 ÷ 2 =

4. 22,048
    + 31,456

10. 19,191
     + 91,999

15. 2011
     x 66

5. 242
    x 33

To find the answer to this riddle, solve the math problem using your calculator. Then turn the calculator so you can read the answer upside down.

What flies but is not a plane, floats but is not a ship, and honks but is not a truck?

Solve:
50 x 7 x 100 + 9 =

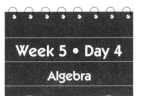

Evaluating Algebraic Expressions

When evaluating an algebraic expression:
First, substitute the numbers for the variables.
Then solve the resulting equation.

Example: $m = 4$ $t = 3$ $7m - 3t =$
$(7 \cdot 4) - (3 \cdot 3)$
$28 - 9$
19

Evaluate the algebraic expressions below using the following values:
$p = 15$, $t = 3$, $r = 2$, $m = 4$.

1. $10 m - (p + 9) - r =$

2. $p (11m + 7t) - 975 =$

3. $2p + 6t + 7r =$

4. $\dfrac{4p}{m - 1}$

5. $\dfrac{6t}{r}$

6. $2tm$

7. $(pt) (rm)$

8. $pr \div 3$

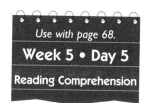

The Disappearing Bees

Around the world, bees are vanishing. Beekeepers open their hives to discover that all the adult bees have vanished, and only the very young bees and the queen remain. While some might argue that the world would be a better place with fewer bees, they would be wrong.

Bees Are Necessary Creatures

First of all, the world needs bees to make honey. Honey is a tasty treat that some people use to sweeten their oatmeal or their tea and sometimes spread on toast. It is known as a "perfect food" because it will never go bad, no matter how long it is left on the shelf. Bees make honey from nectar that they harvest from flowers. Once honey is made, bees store it in honeycombs to save as a food source. Beekeepers collect honey from these honeycombs to sell to human consumers.

Secondly, bees produce wax. Worker bees make beeswax with certain glands in their abdomens. Then, they mold the wax to make the walls of their honeycombs. Beekeepers also gather beeswax. Sometimes the gathered beeswax is used to make candles. These beeswax candles burn much longer than other candles and emit the scent of honey.

The third and most important reason we need bees is for pollination. As bees fly from flower to flower gathering nectar to make honey, they also brush up against pollen, a powdery substance that sticks to their legs. When the bee brushes up against a flower, it leaves some of another plant's pollen on the flower and collects some of the new plant's pollen. This process of moving pollen from plant to plant is called **pollination**. Without pollination, there would be no new flowers. Some of the plants that bees pollinate are fruits and vegetables, which would not be able to reproduce if there were no bees to pollinate them.

Why Are Bees Disappearing?

Many people are concerned about the disappearance of the bees, but there are few clear reasons. Some of the more outlandish theories suggest that electromagnetic radiation from wireless communication devices is the cause. The theory is that as bees find their way back to the hive using an internal compass that is affected by the earth's magnetic field, they become confused by all of the wireless waves in the air and become lost. Most scientists do not give this theory much **credence**. One of the reasons they do not believe the theory is that there is evidence that some bees disappear in rural areas without cell phone towers, and some bees stay in hives on roofs in busy urban centers full of cell phone towers.

Another theory is that a poor diet and stress is causing the bees harm. Ever since the 1950s, some beekeepers have started moving their beehives across the country to search for farmers who need their orchards pollinated. This is called **migratory beekeeping**. These roving beekeepers feed their bees food that would be the equivalent of an energy drink or bar for a person. Some people are concerned that this food is not nutritious enough to keep the bees healthy. Additionally, traveling around in vans is not something that bees are accustomed to in the wild, and so some people suggest that it causes them undue stress. This combination of poor diet and stress might be causing the disappearance.

The most popular theory involves a combination of factors that may include pesticides, infection by tiny mites that carry bacteria, and/or a virus. Scientists are repopulating abandoned colonies with healthy bees to discover if traces of what killed the previous bee population remain. If so, the healthy bees will become sick, too. Then, scientists can study the new bees and possibly determine the causes. Once scientists discover the causes, beekeepers can learn how to counter the threats.

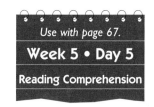

The Disappearing Bees

Answer the following questions that relate to the preceding passage.

1. **Pollination is the way plants—**
   A. attract bees.
   B. reproduce.
   C. repel predators.
   D. make propolis.

2. **First, bees—**
   A. convert nectar into honey.
   B. pollinate plants on their journey.
   C. search for nectar from flowers.
   D. store honey in honeycombs.

3. **Honey is known as a "perfect food" because—**
   A. it is so delicious.
   B. people put it on toast.
   C. bees store it for later.
   D. it never spoils.

4. **Beeswax can be made into ___, which ___**
   A. abdomens; swell up with pus.
   B. candles; smell like honey when they burn.
   C. dolls; frighten little children.
   D. hairbrushes; tangle any hair it touches.

5. **The theory that bees are disappearing because of cell phones is—**
   A. accepted by most scientists.
   B. not accepted by most scientists.
   C. true because bees only disappear near cell phone towers.
   D. true because bees never disappear in places without cell phone towers.

6. **When someone gives an idea credence, they consider that idea—**
   A. worthy of belief.
   B. likely to vanish.
   C. a lie.
   D. capable of producing honey.

7. **Migratory beekeepers—**
   A. send their beehives around the country.
   B. use their bees to pollinate orchards.
   C. sometimes feed their bees something like an energy drink or bar.
   D. all of the above

8. **Most scientists believe bees are disappearing because of—**
   A. radiation from cell phones.
   B. growing cities.
   C. global warming.
   D. none of the above

9. **The most important reason that people need bees is—**
   A. for pollination.
   B. wax.
   C. honey.
   D. no reason, people do not need bees.

10. **If there were no more bees—**
    A. many plants could not be pollinated.
    B. there might be starvation because of a lack of bee-pollinated crops.
    C. some people could no longer get medicine that is made from bee-pollinated plants.
    D. all of the above

11. **One way that scientists are trying to discover what has happened to the bees is by—**

    _____

    _____

    _____

    _____

Here are the skills your middle schooler will be working on this week.

Math
- reading a chart
- using formulas
- geometry: identifying angles
- geometry: measuring angles

Reading
- reading comprehension
- context clues

Writing
- expository writing

Vocabulary
- tricky words

Grammar
- capitalization
- types of sentences

Here is an activity you and your middle schooler might enjoy.

Sign Language Use the manual alphabet chart with your middle schooler to practice spelling out words with your hands. Then figure out the answer to the question at the bottom. Be sure to use the manual alphabet to answer the question.

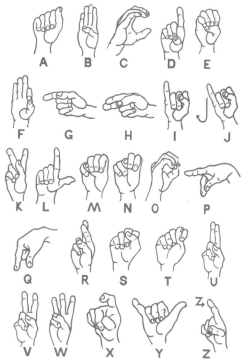

 ?

Your middle schooler might enjoy reading one of the following books:

Summer Ball
by Mike Lupica

Zlata's Diary
by Zlata Filipovic

Oh My Gods! A Look-It-Up Guide to the Gods of Mythology
by Megan E. Bryant

My Week at a Glance

Use this page to set goals and make journal entries.

Goals for Monday_____

_____

Journal: Think about a book you have read that you wish had ended differently.
Describe the ending you wish the book had.

_____

_____

_____

_____

Goals for Tuesday_____

_____

Goals for Wednesday_____

_____

Journal: Imagine you could rename your town. What name would you choose.
Explain your choice.

_____

_____

_____

_____

Goals for Thursday_____

_____

Goals for Friday_____

_____

Journal: Describe what you think the world will be like one hundred years from now.

_____

_____

_____

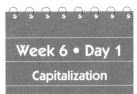

Capitals Aren't Just for States

Read each sentence. Draw three lines under each letter that should be capitalized.

1. The pen name of william sidney porter is o. henry.

2. The declaration of independence was written by thomas jefferson.

3. Many early explorers were spanish, dutch, and english.

4. The golden gate park is located in san francisco, california.

5. mark twain remarked, "when in doubt, tell the truth."

6. dr. elizabeth blackwell was the first woman doctor in america.

7. In crystal city, texas, there is a six-foot-high monument of popeye.

8. Some countries in asia are thailand, india, china, and japan.

9. The store manager, mr. thomas, announced, "we will be closing in five minutes."

10. We went on vacation to florida in july to enjoy disney world.

Read the passage. Draw three lines under each letter that should be capitalized.

What's in a name? An interesting story when it comes to the 50 states in the united states of america! many state names come from indian words. For example, illinois is an algonquin word that means "land of superior men." kansas comes from a sioux word meaning "people of the south wind." several states were named for people. For example, louisiana was named for a king of france, louis xiv. both north carolina and south carolina were named for charles 1, a king of england. washington was named for our first president, george washington. Some states were named for other places. new york was named after york, england, and new jersey takes its name from the isle of jersey off the coast of england. And some states come from spanish. nevada is from a spanish word meaning "snowcapped," and colorado means "ruddy" or "red." How oregon got its name is a bit of a mystery. There are lots of theories, but no one knows for sure.

Counting Calories

A calorie is a unit of energy that humans receive from the food they eat. Do you know how many calories are in some of your favorite foods? The calorie chart below gives average calorie counts for some common foods.

Calorie Chart

	Calories		Calories
1 medium apple	70	1 cup ice cream	270
1 medium banana	100	1 cup skim milk	120
2 slices white bread	140	1 cup whole milk	150
1 regular cheeseburger	518	1 medium orange	65
$\frac{1}{4}$ cup dry, unsweetened cereal	70	1 cup orange juice	120
4 ounces baked chicken	205	1 slice cheese pizza	145
1 cup cola (soda)	145	3 pancakes	180
4 plain sugar cookies	200	1 cup unbuttered popcorn	25
10 French fries	135	15 potato chips	150
1 fried egg	115	1 cup spaghetti and sauce	260
1 hot dog	291	$\frac{3}{4}$ cup tuna fish salad	210

Find Justin's calorie intake for two days. Add each day's calories and then answer the questions.

Day 1   Calories

Breakfast: 3 pancakes   _____
                      1 cup orange juice   _____

Lunch: 20 French fries   _____
                      1 cheeseburger   _____
                      1 cup whole milk   _____
                      4 cookies   _____

Dinner: 3 slices of pizza   _____
                      2 cups soda   _____
                      1 cup ice cream   _____

Snack: 30 potato chips   _____

TOTAL CALORIES   _____

Day 2   Calories

Breakfast: $\frac{1}{4}$ cup dry cereal   _____
                      1 cup skim milk   _____
                      1 cup orange juice   _____

Lunch: $\frac{3}{4}$ cup tuna salad   _____
                      2 slices white bread   _____
                      1 cup skim milk   _____

Dinner: 1 medium apple   _____
                      1 cup spaghetti   _____
                      1 cup skim milk   _____
                      1 medium orange   _____

Snack: 1 cup popcorn   _____

TOTAL CALORIES   _____

On which day did Justin consume fewer calories? _____

What was the difference in calorie intake between days 1 and 2? _____

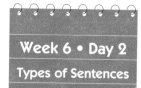

Identifying Types of Sentences

A **simple sentence** has one independent clause and no dependent clauses. It has a subject and a predicate, but these may be compound.

Example: The roller coaster and the terror tower are the most popular rides in the park.

A **compound sentence** has two or more independent clauses joined together, but no dependent clauses. The clauses may be joined by a comma and a coordinating conjunction or by a semicolon. Examples of coordinating conjunctions are **and**, **but**, **or**, **nor**, or **for**.

Example: Frankie wanted to ride the Ferris wheel, **but** Anna was afraid.

A **complex sentence** has one independent clause and one or more dependent clauses. Many dependent clauses are introduced by subordinating conjunctions. Examples of subordinating conjunctions are **after**, **although**, **as**, **as soon as**, **because**, **before**, **even though**, **if**, **since**, **when**, and **until**.

After studying the definitions and examples of the types of sentences, identify each sentence below with **S** for simple, **CD** for compound, and **CX** for complex.

_____ 1. Deja opened her book and raised her hand.

_____ 2. The rain stopped suddenly, and the cold air rushed in from the mountains.

_____ 3. A severe thunderstorm struck the downtown area and interrupted power for hours.

_____ 4. As darkness closed in around the campfire, the campers began to shiver.

_____ 5. When I saw the word in the book, I had to look it up in the dictionary.

_____ 6. Jessica asked the store manager for directions to the new mall.

_____ 7. Mario took the flag down, and Angela folded it.

_____ 8. No one ever entered the old house because people thought it was haunted.

_____ 9. After the baseball game ends, we will eat dinner at a nearby restaurant.

_____ 10. Aldo heard strange noises, but they did not frighten him.

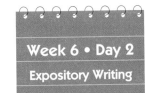

"How To" Prompt

Often the most difficult thing about teaching someone "how-to" do something is being precise and concise with the explanation and step-by-step instructions. Think about your favorite pastime. It may be playing a sport, participating in a hobby, or creating something.

Write a composition that explains to someone else the background of your interest in the activity and how to accomplish it. Be sure that you include all of the details needed to do the activity. When you feel the directions are complete, reread them and make corrections and adjustments. Finally, have someone else read and, if possible, follow your directions. How successful a teacher were you?

How to _____

_____

_____

_____

_____

_____

_____

_____

_____

_____

_____

_____

_____

_____

_____

_____

_____

_____

_____

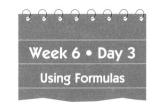

Bone Up on Formulas

To a forensic scientist, a skeleton isn't just a pile of old bones. It's a clue! Sometimes, a scientist may have only one bone to study. But thanks to formulas, even that can be enough to find out information such as how tall the person was when he or she was alive.

Take a look at the real-life forensic formulas below.
Then use them to answer the questions.

Forensic Formulas for Height

In these formulas, r = radius,
h = humerus, and t = tibia.
All measurements are in
centimeters (cm).

Male: $80.4 + 3.7r$ = height
$73.6 + 3.0h$ = height
$81.7 + 2.4t$ = height

Female: $73.5 + 3.9r$ = height
$65.0 + 3.1h$ = height
$72.6 + 2.5t$ = height

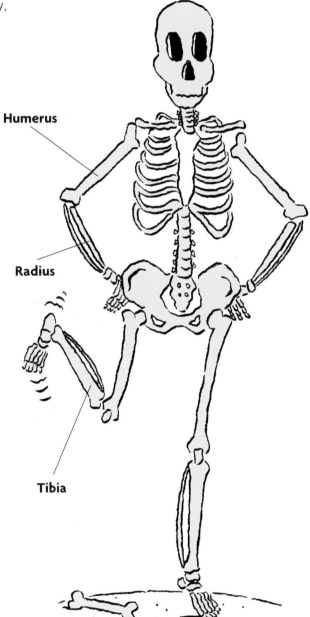

Humerus

Radius

Tibia

1. **A forensic scientist is given the tibia of a woman who lived hundreds of years ago, found at an archaeological dig. What formula should the scientist use to find out how tall the woman was?**

   _____

2. **If the tibia from question 1 was 37 cm long, how tall was the woman?**

   _____

3. **Suppose police find a man's tibia that is 46 cm long. How tall was he?**

   _____

4. **Say a woman's humerus, 28 cm long, is discovered. How tall was she?**_____

5. **A forensic scientist finds a man's radius, 31 cm long. How tall was he?**_____

Confusing Word Choices

Some words are often confused because they sound similar, even though they are not pronounced exactly the same way and have different spellings and meanings. Look closely at the context of each sentence to determine the correct word choice. If needed, use a dictionary.

Underline the word that best completes each sentence.

1. Once the program started, everyone became (quiet, quite).

2. Jennifer cannot decide (wither, whether) to practice her piano lessons or to play soccer.

3. My mother drove (pest, past) Mr. Choo on her way home from work.

4. Dessert is the sweet (course, cores) usually served at the end of a meal.

5. The valedictorian deserved all of the (prize, praise) and adoration she received.

6. Kelly ate the last (peas, piece) of chocolate cake.

7. Everyone on the swim team was able to practice (accept, except) Corey, who was sick.

8. Last summer, we chose to visit Boston, the (capital, capitol) of Massachusetts.

9. Don't forget to bring your camera to take (pitchers, pictures) on our vacation.

10. Of all the people who live on our street, Mrs. Martinez is the loudest (singer, zinger).

11. Isabella saw many (ilk, elk) in Yellowstone National Park this summer.

12. It was interesting to hear about my brother's (signs, science) experiment.

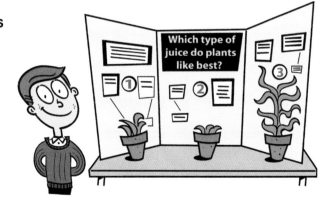

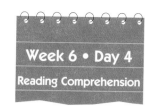

The *Mona Lisa's* Hardships

The *Mona Lisa* is one of the most famous paintings in the world. Leonardo da Vinci painted this portrait of a Renaissance woman in oil on a panel of poplar wood. Although most people are familiar with the lady's smile, they may be surprised at what this painting has survived in its 500 years.

The *Mona Lisa* has seen a great deal in its lifetime. Originally, the portrait hung in the chateau of the King of France, where noblemen and dignitaries could admire it. Later, it graced the wall of Napoleon Bonaparte's bedroom. After the French Revolution, the painting moved to the **Louvre**, an art museum in Paris, France. At the museum, millions of people could come to enjoy the *Mona Lisa's* artistry.

During the Second World War, the *Mona Lisa* was spirited away to safety. It finally landed in Montauben, a city in southern France. Unfortunately, while it was displayed there in 1956, someone splashed acid on it. Later that same year, a man threw a rock at the painting. Both of these acts of **vandalism** led to costly, careful repairs to the painting. The painting now rests at the Louvre behind bulletproof glass to prevent further damage.

By far the most dramatic attack on the *Mona Lisa* occurred when it was stolen in 1911. The police tracked down many leads and investigated everyone from visitors to cleaning staff and security guards. Still, for two long years, they found nothing but dead ends. In 1913, the thief, Vincenzo Peruggia, was caught trying to sell the treasured painting to an antique dealer in Florence, Italy. Finally, the lost lady was found! The painting toured several major cities before being returned to the Louvre, where it remains to this day.

Answer the following questions.

1. **The *Mona Lisa*—**
   A. rests in the Louvre, in Paris, France.
   B. is a painting by Leonardo da Vinci.
   C. is a national treasure for the French.
   D. all of the above.

2. **Da Vinci's *Mona Lisa* is painted—**
   A. on canvas.
   B. on poplar wood.
   C. with pastels.
   D. with a moustache.

3. **When the *Mona Lisa* was hung in the King of France's chateau, it was viewed by—**
   A. millions of people everyday.
   B. Vincenzo Peruggia everyday.
   C. the King only.
   D. noblemen and dignitaries only.

4. **If you made a timeline of the *Mona Lisa's* hardships, which of the following happened first?**
   A. the *Mona Lisa* had a rock thrown at it.
   B. the *Mona Lisa* had acid splashed on it.
   C. the *Mona Lisa* survived World War II.
   D. the *Mona Lisa* was stolen by Peruggia.

5. **The Louvre is—**
   A. the bedroom of Napoleon Bonaparte.
   B. an art museum in Paris, France.
   C. the home of the Mona Lisa.
   D. both B and C

6. **The definition of vandalism is probably—**
   A. careful repairs to paintings.
   B. stealing paintings.
   C. cleaning up property.
   D. willful destruction of property.

Identifying Angles

Angle	Definition	Example
Acute	An angle measuring between 0° and 90	
Obtuse	An angle between 90° and 180°	
Right	An angle measuring exactly 90°	
Straight	An angle of 180°	

Use the chart to help you identify the angles below.

1.

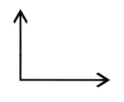

_____

3.

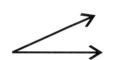

_____

5.

_____

2.

_____

4.

_____

6.

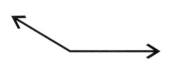

_____

7. An angle measuring between 0° and 90° is _____.

8. An angle measuring exactly 90° is _____.

9. An angle between 90° and 180° is _____.

10. Another name for an angle of 180° is _____.

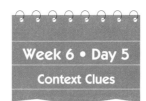

Here's to Your Health!

Everybody wants to be healthy and enjoy all aspects of life. To achieve that goal, there are several factors to be considered.

A healthy diet is essential for a healthy lifestyle. No one food has all the nutrients the body needs to function well, so we need to eat a variety of foods in the proper amounts. Drinking plenty of water is extremely important as it helps maintain a steady body temperature and helps remove wastes from the body. Besides being fun, regular exercise strengthens muscles and keeps them flexible. Getting enough sleep is vital to your health. In most cases, "enough" means between 8 and 12 hours each night. Keeping safe should also always be a top priority. It is foolish to take unnecessary risks. Common sense tells us to avoid tobacco, alcohol, and other drugs. Having a good attitude, being friendly, courteous, and pleasant can also be a sign of good health.

The choices are yours. Will you opt for a healthy lifestyle?

Use words from the passage to solve the puzzle.

Across
3. dangerous chance
4. having soundness of mind and body
7. very important
9. substances body cells use to do their work
10. easily bent

Down
1. first in importance
2. necessary
5. feeling toward a person or thing
6. food eaten
8. to keep away from

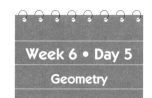

What's Your Angle?

 In order to identify and label angles and angle terms, remember the following:

1) *The vertex of the angle is the point where two rays intersect.*

2) *The two sides of an angle are called rays.*

Example:

3) *Rays are identified by naming the vertex point and the end point of a ray. When you list the two points, be sure to place a line above the letters. $\overline{BA}$ is a ray in the example.*

4) *An angle is formed when two rays share the same end point.*

5) *An angle may be specified or named by using the vertex and a point on each ray.*

6) *The vertex point is always the middle letter of the angle name. In the example, point B is the vertex.*

7) *Using the example, the angle names can be written ∠ ABC, ∠ CBD, ∠ ABD, ∠ DBA, ∠ DBC, or ∠ CBA. You can also use the word angle rather than the ∠ symbol.*

First, answer questions 1–3. Then name all the angles shown in 4 and 5.

1. **In this figure, which point names the vertex?**

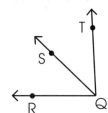

_____

2. **Name the rays in this figure?**

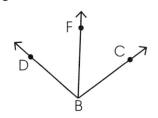

_____

3. **Which group of letters do *not* name an angle in the figure?**

WZY   YZX   XZW   XYZ

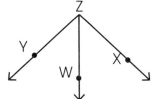

4.

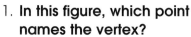

_____
_____
_____
_____

5.

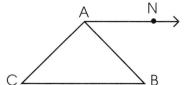

_____
_____
_____

These are the skills your middle schooler will be working on this week.

Math
- geometry: Pythagoras' theorem
- distributive property
- word problems
- measurement

Reading
- reading a chart

Writing
- descriptive writing

Vocabulary
- word origins
- spelling
- dictionary skills

Grammar
- run-on sentences

Here is an activity you and your middle schooler might enjoy.

Game Maker On a rainy summer day when everyone is complaining that there is nothing to do, you may want to challenge your middle schooler to the ancient strategy game of Wari. For 2 players, you will need an empty egg carton (dozen) and 48 playing pieces. Dry beans, paper clips, or any other small, identical pieces all work well. Differentiate the 2 players' pieces (by type or color) so that you have two distinguishable sets of 24 pieces each.

To Play: 1) Each player begins with 24 markers and chooses one side of the carton. Then, each player places 4 markers in each of the 6 cups on his/her side of the board. The object of the game is to be the first player to capture the majority of the pieces. **2)** Play moves counter clockwise. Player #1 takes all of the pieces from any hole on his/her side of the board and places 1 piece in each of the next 4 holes. **3)** During a turn, if the last piece of a move is placed in an opponent's hole containing 2 or 3 pieces, the player capturers all of the pieces. Additionally, the player wins the pieces in the adjacent holes if they contain 2 or 3 pieces. Captured pieces are removed from play. **4)** When a hole contains 12 or more pieces, the player must "sow" them to different holes, always skipping the hole from which they were taken. **5)** When a player has 6 empty holes and the opponent cannot fill them, the player wins all the pieces left on the board. **To Win the Game:** Empty all of your holes first and capture the most pieces.

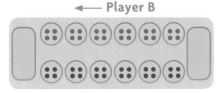

← Player B

Player A →

Your middle schooler might enjoy reading one of the following books:

Year of Impossible Goodbyes
by Sook Nyul Choi

Jacob Have I Loved
by Katherine Paterson

Napoleon: Emperor and Conqueror
by Kimberley Heuston

My Week at a Glance

Use this page to set goals and make journal entries.

Goals for Monday_____

_____

Journal: Imagine that you are able to "swap" places with one of your parents for a day. What rules would you make for him or her? How would you act differently than he or she typically does?

_____

_____

_____

_____

Goals for Tuesday_____

_____

Goals for Wednesday_____

_____

Journal: The post office creates postage stamps to commemorate people and events. Imagine you are commissioned to choose a person to be honored. Whom would you choose and why?

_____

_____

_____

_____

Goals for Thursday_____

_____

Goals for Friday_____

_____

Journal: While walking along a beach, you find and uncork an old bottle. What happens next?

_____

_____

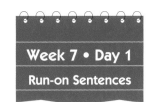

Going On and On . . .

In a **run-on** sentence, two (or more) sentences are written as though they were one sentence, and a comma is placed where a period should be. There are three ways to correct a run-on sentence: You can write two simple sentences; you can write one compound sentence; or you can write one complex sentence.

Example: Alex plays the guitar, Lisa plays the violin.

Two Sentences: Alex plays the guitar. Lisa plays the violin.

Compound Sentence: Alex plays the guitar, **and** Lisa plays the violin.

Complex Sentence: Alex plays the guitar, **while** Lisa plays the violin.

Correct each run-on sentence by writing two simple sentences, or one compound sentence, or a complex sentence.

1. We have been practicing our soccer plays every day we really enjoy doing this.

_____

2. Joshua dribbled the basketball he took a jump shot.

_____

3. My sister's new watch is waterproof our mother wears it when she goes for a swim.

_____

4. Here is your birthday present do not open it until your birthday.

_____

5. Theresa is planning a surprise party Samantha does not suspect a thing.

_____

6. Aunt Martha wrote a letter to her brother Dad mailed the letter today for her.

_____

7. Leandra is walking to the park Dianne is riding her bike.

_____

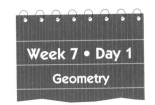
Pythagoras' Theorem

The **Pythagorean Theorem** is a simple rule about the proportion of sides of right angle triangles. In a right triangle, the square of the hypotenuse equals the sum of the square of the other sides. More commonly stated as $a^2 + b^2 = c^2$.

The Pythagorean Theorem can be used any time you know the length of two sides of a right triangle to find the length of the third side.

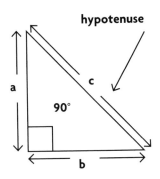

Example:

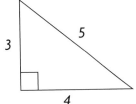

$a^2 + b^2 = c^2$

$3^2 + 4^2 = 5^2$

$9 + 16 = 25$

$25 = 25$

Remember to calculate the square root to determine the actual length of the third side: $\sqrt{25} = 5$

Use the Pythagorean Theorem to determine the hypotenuse of the following right triangles. Show your work. Use a calculator to help you figure out the square root.

1. One side of a right triangle is 9 feet. The other side is 12 feet. What is the length of the hypotenuse?

_____

2. If one side of a triangle is 20 feet and the other side is 21 feet, what is the hypotenuse?

_____

3. A large city park is triangular in shape. The north-south and east-west streets meet in a right or 90° angle, given that the north-south side is 5 blocks long and the east-west side is 12 blocks long and that all blocks surrounding the park are of equal lengths. What is the approximate number of blocks forming the diagonal street?

$a^2 + b^2 = c^2$

$5^2 + 12^2 = c^2$

Solve for the value of c.

Answer: c = _____

The Pythagorean Theorem can also be used to tell whether a right triangle can be formed from three given line segments.

4. Can a right triangle be formed with sides of 6 feet, 8 feet, and 12 feet?

$a^2 + b^2 = c^2$

$6^2 + 8^2 = 12^2$

Answer: _____

5. What if the sides were 6, 8, and 10 meters?

Answer: _____

Words From Other Languages

Many words in English come from other languages. Some examples are given in the chart below.

Other Language	Word	Definition
Dutch	aloof	unfriendly, detached
	bicker	argue, squabble
French	clique	group, gang
	niche	place, position
Arabic	tariff	tax, duty
	zenith	top, pinnacle
Italian	torso	upper part of the human body
	regatta	series of boat races
Hindi	loot	rob, ransack
	bungalow	small house, cottage

Read each question. Choose the best answer from the words in the chart above.

1. **Which of these would you not want to do with a friend?**
   bicker   niche   regatta

2. **Which of these would be fun to watch?**
   tariff   regatta   bungalow

3. **Which of these might you live in?**
   loot   bungalow   clique

4. **Which of these words describes what winning the World Series is for a baseball team?**
   zenith   torso   clique

5. **Which of the following has a torso?**
   guidebook   spider   human being

Read each set of words below. Cross out the one word in each group that is not a synonym.

6. **gang**   **group**   **sound**   **clique**

7. **pinnacle**   **top**   **zenith**   **loss**

8. **instrument**   **loot**   **rob**   **ransack**

9. **argue**   **bicker**   **slot**   **fight**

10. **tariff**   **tax**   **delay**   **duty**

85

Have No Fear

Don't worry—algebra is nothing to fear!
But some people do fear specific things,
like heights, snakes, or fire. These strong
fears are called phobias.

To find out what each phobia below means,
use the distributive property to simplify each
expression. Draw a line to match the
expression to its simplest form.

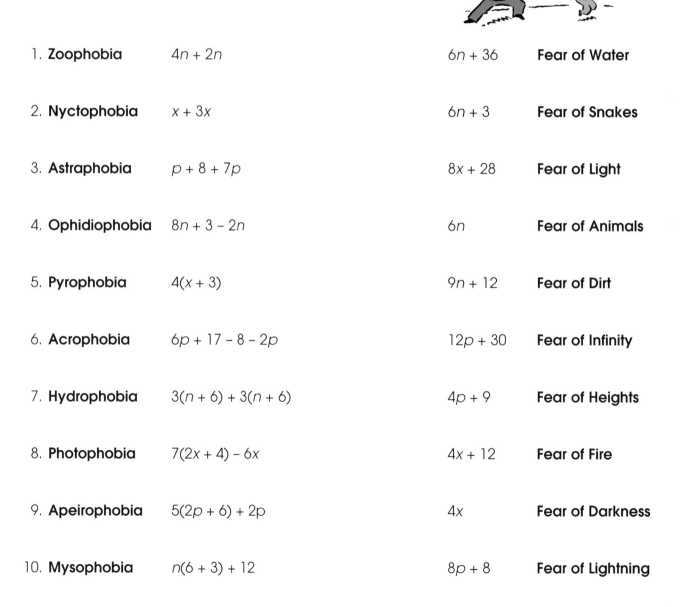

1. **Zoophobia**	$4n + 2n$		$6n + 36$	**Fear of Water**
2. **Nyctophobia**	$x + 3x$		$6n + 3$	**Fear of Snakes**
3. **Astraphobia**	$p + 8 + 7p$		$8x + 28$	**Fear of Light**
4. **Ophidiophobia**	$8n + 3 - 2n$		$6n$	**Fear of Animals**
5. **Pyrophobia**	$4(x + 3)$		$9n + 12$	**Fear of Dirt**
6. **Acrophobia**	$6p + 17 - 8 - 2p$		$12p + 30$	**Fear of Infinity**
7. **Hydrophobia**	$3(n + 6) + 3(n + 6)$		$4p + 9$	**Fear of Heights**
8. **Photophobia**	$7(2x + 4) - 6x$		$4x + 12$	**Fear of Fire**
9. **Apeirophobia**	$5(2p + 6) + 2p$		$4x$	**Fear of Darkness**
10. **Mysophobia**	$n(6 + 3) + 12$		$8p + 8$	**Fear of Lightning**

Writing to a Prompt

Do you dream of the beach or the mountains when you think of a perfect vacation? Perhaps you cannot decide between the two but can think of a perfect spot where the two come together. Even if you have never visited your dream location, you have seen pictures and/or videos that make you long to go there.

Choose a location. Describe the scenery. How does it look? What feelings does the place evoke? What are the smells and sounds that are unique to your special place?

Describe this special place in as much detail as possible so that the reader can be transported there in their mind's eye.

A Dream Vacation

_____

_____

_____

_____

_____

_____

_____

_____

_____

_____

_____

Selecting Correctly Spelled Nouns

First, read the sentence. Then circle the correctly spelled noun (names a person, place, or thing) to complete the sentence.

1. **We live in an _____.**   A. apartment   B. apartmint   C. apartmant

2. **Jose plays the _____.**   A. banjoe   B. bannjo   C. banjo

3. **Mark is scared of his own _____.**   A. shaddow   B. shadow   C. shadowe

4. **In which _____ did she go?**   A. dirktion   B. direcshun   C. direction

5. **Do you know their _____?**   A. sloggan   B. slogan   C. slogen

6. **Mom cannot find her _____.**   A. almanak   B. almanac   C. allmanac

7. **Did you bring your _____?**   A. pajamas   B. pagamas   C. pajammas

8. **An _____ is very important.**   A. education   B. edjucation   C. edducation

9. **The doctor checked my _____.**   A. vizion   B. vishun   C. vision

10. **At the zoo I want to see the _____.**   A. rinocerhos   B. rhinoceros   C. rinoceros

11. **The _____ was sold today.**   A. merchandise   B. mershendise   C. merchandize

12. **Jill is a _____ for the group.**   A. volunteer   B. voluntear   C. volunteir

13. **The _____ is quite valuable.**   A. diamend   B. dimond   C. diamond

14. **The house _____ is ringing.**   A. tellephone   B. telephone   C. telaphone

15. **The _____ was a forgery.**   A. documint   B. documant   C. document

16. **My parents' _____ is Monday.**   A. anniversary   B. aniversary   C. anniversery

17. **Our _____ starts tomorrow.**   A. vakation   B. vacation   C. vacatiun

18. **Please seal the _____.**   A. envelope   B. invelop   C. envelop

19. **The _____ frightened Judith.**   A. thundar   B. thunder   C. thundir

20. **May I borrow your _____?**   A. handkerchief   B. hankerchief   C. hankerchef

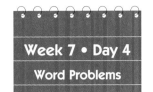

Major League Baseball Word Problems

So you think you know about baseball. Take a look back at some facts and figures related to major league baseball in the late 1990s. When you have solved these problems, you may want to research present-day major league facts and figures and compare these statistics.

1. In the late 1990s, there were 30 teams in the major league. The average team had 33 players. How many players could potentially be in the league?

2. In 1998, the average team revenue was $84,383,533. In 1997, the revenues were 7% less. What was the 1977 revenue, rounded to the nearest dollar?

3. Daily attendance at games varies according to the day of the week and whether the game is played during the day or at night. One team reported their average daily attendance was 46,783 fans. During that time, the average ticket price for a game was $14.55. What would have been the average daily income from ticket sales that year rounded to the nearest dollar?

4. Not all teams enjoyed the same levels of attendance. In 1998, the team with the lowest daily average saw only 11,295 tickets on average sold per day. As a result of lower attendance figures, the cost per ticket was under $10, only $9.81 per ticket. How much less did that team take in per day than the team in problem 3? Round to the nearest dollar.

5. The team with the highest revenue also had the highest salaries. The team's revenue was $170,236,000 and paid $88,236,708 in salaries. Once payroll was met, what revenue did the team have?

6. One rookie made $325,000 in 1998 and played 162 games. What was his average per game income? Round to the nearest dollar.

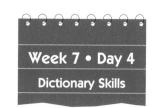

Decisions, Decisions

Write "true" or "false" for each statement below. Then, on another sheet of paper, rewrite each "false" sentence so it becomes a "true" sentence. Use a dictionary to look up the underlined word if necessary.

1. It is reasonable to <u>accelerate</u> as you approach a stop sign. _____

2. You need <u>stamina</u> to run in a marathon. _____

3. <u>Perishable</u> food will last for a long time. _____

4. You expect to win the prize if you do <u>mediocre</u> work. _____

5. An umpire is a good <u>utensil</u>. _____

6. A bag of potato chips is a <u>wholesome</u> breakfast. _____

7. You should stack cans for a display in a <u>haphazard</u> manner. _____

8. It would be <u>frivolous</u> to buy a new pair of shoes because the soles are worn through. _____

9. Going to the mall in a horse and buggy is <u>obsolete</u>. _____

10. You are being <u>punctual</u> when you arrive at the doctor's office at 2:25 P.M. for your 2:30 P.M. appointment. _____

11. You could expect to see <u>boisterous</u> behavior at a carnival. _____

12. You are being helpful when you <u>defy</u> your mother. _____

13. You would expect a gymnast to be <u>nimble</u>. _____

14. Going to Grandmother's house for Thanksgiving is a <u>predicament</u>. _____

15. You are <u>persistent</u> because you tried to solve the crossword puzzle for only five minutes. _____

Burning Calories

Number of Minutes Needed to Burn Specific Calories

FOOD	Per Serving Calories	Running	Swimming	Biking	Walking	Aerobics
Apple	70	5	9	11	18	11
Cereal	70	5	9	11	18	11
Cheeseburger	518	39	64	82	136	78
Cola	145	11	18	23	38	22
French Fries	135	10	17	21	36	20
Ice Cream	270	20	33	43	71	41
Orange Juice	120	9	15	19	32	18
Pizza	145	11	18	23	38	22
Popcorn	25	2	3	4	7	4
Potato Chips	150	11	19	24	39	23

Based on the chart, answer the following questions.

1. If Corey drinks a glass of orange juice, how many minutes must he swim to burn it off?

   _____

2. It will take Tonio _____ minutes of swimming to burn off a package of potato chips.

3. Amarani can walk off a slice of pizza in _____ minutes.

4. Kody needs to burn off the calories in a cheeseburger and French fries. He can run for _____ minutes or bike for _____ minutes.

5. Pauline can choose either to do aerobics for _____ minutes or to bike for _____ minutes to burn off the calories in a dish of ice cream.

6. How many minutes will it take Jordan to run off the calories in two slices of pizza?_____

7. David chose an apple and popcorn for his snack. How many calories were in his two snacks?_____

8. Carlos wants to do whatever exercise will burn his extra calories the fastest. Which exercise should he do?_____

Measurement Review

Complete each sentence below to review what you know about units of customary measure.

1. Another name for 1,000 years is a _____.

2. A small car might weigh about 1 _____.

3. A fortnight has 14 _____.

4. The abbreviation _____ is used for the unit that has 12 inches.

5. $\frac{1}{24}$ of a day is called an _____.

6. The abbreviation for the unit that is $\frac{1}{8}$ of a cup is _____.

7. $\frac{1}{36}$ of a yard is called an _____.

8. A _____ contains 8 fluid ounces.

9. The distance 10,560 feet is equal to 2 _____.

10. Another way to say 12:00 P.M. is _____.

11. Four pints is equal to a _____.

12. There are _____ years in a decade.

13. $\frac{1}{4}$ of a gallon is called a _____.

14. $\frac{1}{128}$ of a gallon is called an _____.

15. A mile has 1,760 _____.

16. There are 3,600 seconds in 1 _____.

17. There are _____ units in 2 dozen.

18. The abbreviation for the weight equivalent to $\frac{1}{1000}$ of a ton is _____.

Helping Your Middle Schooler Get Ready: Week 8

These are the skills your middle schooler will be working on this week.

Math
- algebra: inequalities
- algebra: patterns
- problem solving

Reading
- reading comprehension
- reading for details

Writing
- research skills
- business letter

Vocabulary
- analogies

Grammar
- punctuation: semicolons
- subject-verb agreement

Here are some activities you and your middle schooler might enjoy.

Make a Coupon Book Have your child make a book of "coupons" that entitle the bearer to goods or services he or she is willing to provide. Remind your child to include any "restrictions" or "expiration dates." Read actual coupons for examples of terms and conditions to include.

Thinking Beyond the Page Your middle schooler has probably been reading several books over the summer. Consider asking, "What do you think about the book so far?" "What do you think will happen next in the book?" Encourage your child to discuss interests and observations about the books he or she is reading.

Your middle schooler might enjoy reading one of the following books:

The Trumpeter of Krakow
by Eric P. Kelly

To Kill a Mockingbird
by Harper Lee

Zach's Lie
by Roland Smith

Coupon
Entitles holder to one free night of
Baby Sitting
Expires May 31

My Week at a Glance

Use this page to set goals and make journal entries.

Goals for Monday_____
_____

Journal: Smells have the ability to delight or repel us. Make a list of several different smells;
then describe your reactions to each of them.

_____
_____
_____

Goals for Tuesday_____
_____

Goals for Wednesday_____
_____

Journal: A local recycling company is sponsoring a repurposing contest. The person who
develops the most creative uses for a shoe box wins the contest. Think of several uses for
an empty shoe box and describe your winning entry.

_____
_____
_____
_____

Goals for Thursday_____
_____

Goals for Friday_____
_____

Journal: An old saying advises that "those who live in glass houses should never throw
stones." What would life be like living in a glass house?

_____
_____
_____

Amazing Animal Inequalities

Below you'll find some incredible facts about animals. But only some of them are true!
To find out which statements are just hogwash, look at each inequality. If the inequality is true,
so is the fact. Circle True. If the inequality is false, the statement is, too. Circle False.

1. **Some types of bats measure just one inch long.**
   $2x - 14 \leq 8$, $x = 11$

   True   False

2. **The amazing cheetah can run 120 miles per hour.**
   $3p - 12 > 0$, $p = 4$

   True   False

3. **A giant South American species of rabbit can weigh up to 275 pounds.**
   $r + 14 - 2r \leq 12$, $r = 1$

   True   False

4. **Blue whales weigh as much as 260,000 pounds.**
   $20 > 7 + 4j$, $j = 2$

   True   False

5. **Koalas are the laziest animals in the world. They snooze 22 hours per day.**
   $4y + 6 + 3y < 50$, $y = 6$

   True   False

6. **Some clams live up to 200 years.**
   $15 \geq 18 - 3z$, $z = 1$

   True   False

7. **One of the top ten names for pet goldfish in the U.S. is "Fluffy."**
   $u \div 12 \geq 3$, $u = 24$

   True   False

8. **There are at least 1,000,000 insects for every human being on Earth!**
   $16 < 3t + 8$, $t = 3$

   True   False

Semicolons

Let's review how to use semicolons.

Use a **semicolon** . . .

- between the clauses of compound sentences if they are not joined by a conjunction.
  Example: Baseball is a sport; it can be an occupation.

- between clauses that are joined by certain transitional words and phrases in a compound sentence (accordingly, consequently, for example, for instance, furthermore, however, moreover, nevertheless, otherwise, and therefore.)
  Example: We will have the patio door installed this Friday afternoon; otherwise, we will have to wait until next week.

- between the items in a series if the items already contain commas. Naturally, this will avoid a confusing number of commas.
  Example: The presidential candidate toured Nashville, Tennessee; Atlanta, Georgia; Mobile, Alabama; and Miami, Florida.

Insert semicolons in the following sentences.

1. My brother Mark will attend college this fall however, he has to earn money this summer.

2. When my uncle was on tour, he visited the following cities: Chicago, Illinois St. Louis, Missouri Billings, Montana and San Francisco, California.

3. The player scored a goal the fans screamed enthusiastically.

4. It snowed all day therefore, we stayed inside the house.

5. My brother loved the latest action film I found it boring.

6. I'll ask Dad to drive us to the mall otherwise, we will have to walk.

7. Jana is bringing cups, soda, and ice to the party Walter is bringing music and Sammy is bringing fruit and popcorn.

8. Band practice was postponed until Saturday however, I have soccer practice that day.

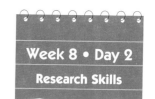
Common Knowledge Quiz

How many of the following trivia questions can you answer? If necessary, use an encyclopedia, atlas, almanac, or the Internet.

1. What six U.S. states were named for English kings and queens?_____

_____

_____

2. True or false: Giraffes sleep standing up?_____

3. How many vertebrae do most mammals have in their necks?_____

4. What is the wettest spot in the United States?_____

5. What is the driest spot in the United States?_____

6. How many carats are in pure gold?_____

7. The longest snake is the _____.

8. True or false: The chemical composition of the Sun is mostly gas?_____

9. Which human bone is the longest in the body?_____

10. Are gorillas carnivorous?_____

11. Which American presidents were born in Texas?_____

12. What do the initials in *R.S.V.P.* stand for?_____

_____

13. How many legs does a spider have? How many eyes?_____

14. Who was the first American president to be awarded the Nobel Peace Prize?_____

15. Which river is the longest in the world?_____

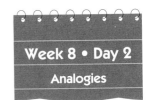

Word Relationships

 Analogies *show relationships between words.*
Analogies are read, "comma is to pause as period is to stop."
They are written using symbols, as follows: comma : pause :: period : stop

Read the first pair of words; then add the word that best completes the second pair of words.

1. **basketball : hands :: soccer :** _____

2. **sociable : extrovert :: retiring :** _____

3. **prohibit : allow :: strenuous :** _____

4. **sterile : clean :: muddy :** _____

5. **cafeteria : school :: kitchen :** _____

6. **green : color :: carrot :** _____

7. **diver : descend :: climber :** _____

8. **jaguar : cat :: duck :** _____

9. **Nile : river :: Egypt :** _____

10. **jazz : music :: ballet :** _____

11. **summer : season :: week :** _____

12. **commence : begin :: cease :** _____

13. **teeth : chew :: eyes :** _____

14. **money : buy :: advertisement :** _____

15. **eat : ate :: find :** _____

16. **towel : dry :: scissors :** _____

Do They Agree?

 A verb must agree with its subject in number. **Number** *refers to whether a word is singular (naming one) or plural (naming more than one).*

In each sentence, underline the subject. Then underline the correct verb form in the parentheses.

1. Most stories in a newspaper (begin, begins) with a lead paragraph.

2. The lead of most stories (answer, answers) the questions *who, what, when, where,* and *why.*

3. What (cause, causes) a volcano to erupt?

4. A volcano (don't, doesn't) usually erupt without warning.

5. The word *volcano* (come, comes) from the Latin word *vulcan.*

6. Occasionally, a volcano (has, have) blown a mountain apart.

7. Everyone (want, wants) to know about the Loch Ness monster.

8. Many (look, looks) for it in the waters of the lake in Scotland.

9. Some (think, thinks) the monster is a prehistoric beast.

10. Bar magnets (am, is, are) used as the needles in compasses.

11. The needle in a bar magnet (am, is, are) attracted to the North Pole.

12. Square dancing (grew, grown) out of other forms of folk dancing.

13. Directions to the dancers are (sang, sung) by a square dance caller.

14. Even if you (knew, known) nothing about dancing, you could learn the steps.

15. Will your friend (join, joins) you for the square dance?

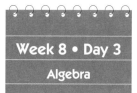

Missing Museums

Meet Anne DeSplay. She just loves museums! Anne was planning a trip to see some of her favorite museums in the U.S., but she got them all mixed up. Now, Anne needs your help!

To find out where each real museum is located, figure out what number completes each number pattern. Find your answer in the Museum Locations box and write it following the pattern. Then, explain the relationship within each pattern.

Museum Names

1. **Tupperware Historic Food Container Museum**

   224, 112, 56, 28,... _____

   _____

2. **Museum of Bad Art**

   11, 24, 37, 50,... _____

_____

	Museum Locations
27	Lincoln, Nebraska
63	Boston, Massachusetts
14	Orlando, Florida
34	Dallas, Texas
125	Wichita, Kansas
129	Phoenix, Arizona

3. **Hall of Flame (Fire Fighting Museum)**

   5, 9, 17, 33, 65,... _____

_____

4. **Leroy's Motorcycle Museum**

   1, 5, 13, 29, 61,... _____

_____

5. **National Museum of Roller Skating**

   48, 47, 45, 42, 38, 33,... _____

_____

6. **Tolbert's Chili Parlor and Museum of Chili**

   1, 1, 2, 3, 5, 8, 13, 21,... _____

_____

It's All Business

There are many reasons for writing a business letter. You might request information, express an opinion to a public official, or explain a problem with something you have bought. A business letter has six parts.

*Your address and the date go in the **heading**. The name and address of the person or company receiving the letter go in the **inside address**.*

*A **formal greeting** comes next. This includes a title of respect, such as Dear Mr., Dear Mrs., Dear Ms., Dear Sir, etc.*

*The **body** states the purpose of your letter.*

*A **formal closing,** such as Sincerely yours, follows the body. Your **signature** is last.*

Imagine that you ordered the Thingamabob, a popular new toy from the Razzle-Dazzle Toy Company, for $29.99. It was a gift for your younger brother. Unfortunately, the toy broke the first time he played with it! How would you feel? Would you want your money back? Would you want another Thingamabob? Write a letter to Mr. Dewey Cheatem, the president of the company at 123 Any Street, Anytown, Anystate, 00001. Explain why you are writing. Tell what happened and how. Then suggest a solution to the problem.

heading ⟶ _____

_____

_____

_____ ⟵ inside address

_____

_____

body

_____ : ⟵ formal greeting

↓

_____

_____

_____

_____

_____

_____

_____

formal closing ⟶ _____

signature ⟶ _____

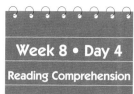
Strange New World

Amira opened her eyes. It wasn't a dream. A moment ago she was in her bland living room with her friend Cesar, playing an old video game. Now that bland room was gone.

She and Cesar stood in a crudely rendered world of primary colors. Everything looked blocky, like it was made of large colored bricks. There were green blocks underfoot, blue and white blocks in the sky. A blocky turtle waddled past them. Suddenly, she realized, *they are all made of pixels!* Cesar laughed.

He took off, sprinting down the blocky green path. Amira had to dash to keep up with him. He stopped so suddenly that she almost ran into him. Before she could catch her breath, he pointed up at what had caught his eye.

It was a big yellow block, as tall as either of them, inexplicably **suspended** in the air about ten feet above them. They could see no wires.

Before she could stop him, Cesar leapt up into the air. This new world had granted them new abilities, too, because he flew up three times the height he normally could and head-butted the floating block.

CLINK! A giant coin shot out of the top of the block. Amira tried to move out of the way, but the coin was plummeting toward her. She cringed. As soon as it touched her, the coin faded harmlessly. She exhaled softly.

Cesar pointed down the path where more yellow blocks waited in a row. He held out his hand. Amira looked from his outstretched hand to the blocky path ahead, then back at his beaming face. She took a deep breath. She smiled, reached out, and took his hand.

Answer the following questions.

1. **This story takes place—**
   A. on Mars.
   B. at a barbecue.
   C. in a living room.
   D. in a video game.

2. **First, Amira—**
   A. opens her eyes.
   B. takes Cesar's hand.
   C. smiled.
   D. plays a video game.

3. **CLINK! is an example of the literary term—**
   A. onomatopoeia.
   B. alliteration.
   C. allusion.
   D. foreshadowing.

4. **Suspended is used in this story to mean—**
   A. to hang in midair.
   B. to sprint down the path.
   C. to be temporarily forced to leave school.
   D. to spur to action.

5. **When Cesar sees the _____, he _____**
   A. blocky turtle; catches it.
   B. giant coin; runs away.
   C. big yellow block; head-butts it.
   D. green blocky path; collapses.

6. **The blocks making up the world are—**
   A. coins.
   B. pixels.
   C. atoms.
   D. friends.

What, No Numbers?

The problems below have no numbers. Decide how you would solve each one. Tell what you would add, subtract, multiply, or divide to find the answer. If it helps you, fill in reasonable numbers.

1. Max saved some money by buying a book of 10 movie passes rather than individual tickets. How can he figure out how much money he saved?

_____

_____

2. Inez knows the number of miles she ran last week. She knows how many hours she ran. How can she figure out her rate of speed in miles per hour?

_____

_____

3. Ed knows his car's odometer readings (in miles) before and after a trip. He knows the number of gallons of gasoline he used. How can he figure out the number of miles-per-gallon his car got on the trip?

_____

_____

4. Pat knows the weight and price of two different-size boxes of dry cat food. How can he figure out which of the two is the better buy?

_____

_____

5. Li has a paper route. She delivers a certain number of papers every day. For each paper she delivers, she makes the same amount of money. How can she figure out her hourly wage?

_____

_____

Forests on Fire

There are some places where you can expect wildfires. In California, fires burn 50,000 to 500,000 acres of land every year. Some of the plants that live there have oily sap. They can survive the dry, hot summers, but if they catch fire they explode into flame. Grasses grow thick during the spring rains and then die. They dry into a thick layer of straw that burns fast, making a very hot fire.

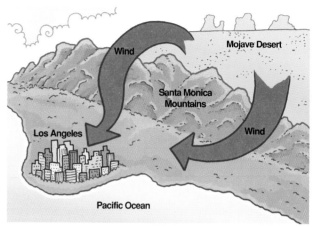

Winds blow over the dry Mojave Desert and travel toward the Pacific Ocean.

Fires can start wherever there's fuel to burn. Southern California has plenty of fuel and a hot, dry wind that blows every year between mid-September and late October. This wind, called the Santa Ana, passes over the inland desert, losing moisture and gaining heat, and rushes toward the ocean to the west. The Santa Ana wind fans the flames and makes fighting the fires nearly impossible.

Forests are a natural storehouse of fuel for a fire. During a dry summer, dead trees and low brush in a forest can burst into flame wherever lightning strikes. Rain usually puts out these fires. But sometimes the combination of dry fuel, hot dry air, and strong winds is just right for a major forest fire.

In 1988, Wyoming's Yellowstone National Park was burned by several such fires at once. Lightning struck in two places. A worker dropped a lit cigarette in another place. On the worst day of the fire, more than 600 square kilometers (about 230 square miles) of forest burned. Clouds of smoke that looked like storm clouds rose into the atmosphere. Smoke blocked the sun and drifted far beyond the park.

Firefighters work hard to control fires like those in Yellowstone and California, many of which are caused by people. But long before humans learned how to start or put out a fire, prairies and forests burned every year. Both kinds of land recovered, as they have in Yellowstone and in California.

1. **What mountains are between Los Angeles and the Mojave Desert?**_____

2. **What path do the Santa Ana winds follow?**_____

3. **Why might a rainy spring increase the risk of forest fires?**

_____

4. **In 1988, what caused the fires in Yellowstone National Park?**

_____

5. **True or false: Yellowstone is located in California:** _____

These are the skills your middle schooler will be working on this week.

Math
- logic and problem solving
- real-world math
- finding averages
- metric system

Reading
- reading comprehension

Writing
- narrative writing

Vocabulary
- idioms

Grammar
- prepositions
- types of sentences

Here is an activity you and your middle schooler might enjoy.

Container Gardening You do not have to be a farmer or even have an outdoor space to grow beautiful flowers or delicious vegetables. You and your child can create a container garden regardless of where you live. To start, you will need to gather the following: a large container, such as a flower or window box, a planter, wooden box, or even several large coffee cans; potting soil; small stones or pebbles; some type of under tray, and water. Choose a sunny place, such as a windowsill. You will also need a few seedlings (small plants) or seeds.

Follow these simple steps: First, select what you want to grow. Herbs, such as parsley and chives, a cherry tomato plant, radishes, chilies, and/or flowers, such as impatiens and geraniums, all do well indoors. Next, punch a few drainage holes in the bottom of your container. Line the bottom with an even layer of pebbles or small stones. Fill the container with potting soil. When planting seedlings, plant them so that the roots have plenty of room to spread. Plant seeds according to package directions (not too deep, though). Set the container on the tray and place in the sun. Be sure to water the plants so that the soil is moist, not soggy. Finally, keep the soil moist and turn the container to keep the plants or flowers growing strong.

Your middle schooler might enjoy reading one of the following books:

The Hero and the Crown
by Robin McKinley

Night of the Twisters
by Ivy Ruckman

Harriet Tubman: Secret Agent
by Thomas B. Allen

 # My Week at a Glance

Use this page to set goals and make journal entries.

Goals for Monday_____

_____

Journal: A winning lottery ticket is sure to change a person's life. What would you do with a major lottery win? How would you spend the money?

_____

_____

_____

_____

Goals for Tuesday_____

Goals for Wednesday_____

_____

Journal: You have been chosen to create a new museum. What kind of exhibits would you include? Who would be your intended audience?

_____

_____

_____

_____

Goals for Thursday_____

Goals for Friday_____

Journal: Do animals have thoughts and feelings? Support your position, either pro or con.

_____

_____

_____

Let's Be Reasonable

Just exactly where is the middle of nowhere? To find out, first circle the best answer for each statement. Then write the letter of the correct answer in the code at the bottom.

1. **California is the state with the largest population, about _____.**
   V. 3,900   W. 39 million   X. 390 million

2. **On the other hand, Wyoming has a population of about _____.**
   T. 540,000   U. 54,000   V. 5,400

3. **The border between Canada and the United States is _____ miles long.**
   L. 550,000   M. 55,000   N. 5,500

4. **The lowest point in the nation, Death Valley, is _____ feet below sea level.**
   N. 0.282   O. 282   P. 2,820

5. **The height of Mt. McKinley, the highest in the country, is _____ feet.**
   D. 2,320   E. 20,320   F. 200,320

6. **Yellowstone, the first national park, was founded in _____.**
   A. 1872   B. 1802   C. 1772

7. **The smallest state, Rhode Island, has an area of _____ square miles.**
   S. 1,545   T. 41,545   U. 241,545

8. **Texas, the second largest, has an area of _____ square miles.**
   G. 86,861   H. 268,601   I. 6,168,601

9. **Crater Lake, the deepest lake in the nation, is _____ feet deep.**
   L. 32   M. 932   N. 1,943

10. **Oklahoma has the largest Native American population, about _____.**
    Q. 2,500   R. 250,000   S. 25 million

11. **The number of Americans under age 18 is about _____.**
    H. 1 million   I. 65 million   J. 200 million

| __ | __ | __ | __ | __ | __ | __ | __ | __ | , | __ | __ |
| 6 | 11 | 3 | 7 | 1 | 4 | 10 | 2 | 8 | | 9 | 5 |

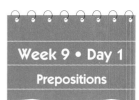

Preposition Crossword Puzzle

Find the preposition in each sentence. Then place the preposition where it belongs in the puzzle.

Across

1. Jennifer went with her best friend.
3. The dog ran after the cat.
4. Pirates hid the gold below the deck.
6. Kathy and Bobby went to the store.
8. The tan colt walked behind his mother.
9. Practice the piano until 4:00.
11. The balloon flew above the trees.

Down

1. Do not go swimming without a buddy.
2. Your turn to bat is before Jose.
3. Carl went around the corner.
4. The child may not go beyond the gate.
5. The ladder leaned against the wall.
7. Mr. Parker's farm is over the next hill.
9. Look for the ball under the fence.
10. Please put the puzzle upon the table.

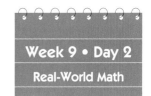

Shop 'Til You Drop

How much do shoppers who buy in bulk really save? Do some research to find out. Visit a store or look at newspaper ads to find some of the items listed below. Add some items of your own to the table. Then complete the table to find out if you're shopping smart.

Item	Cost of Single Item	Cost of Multipack	Number of Items in Multipack	Savings
Paper Towels				
Canned Dog Food				
Bars of Soap				
Ballpoint Pens				
Canned Soda				

Identifying Sentence Types

 A **simple sentence** *has a subject and a verb, and expresses a complete thought. It does not include any dependent clauses, but it may have compound parts (i.e., subjects and verbs).*

Examples: *Johnny read his research paper. Johnny and Marcia read and compared their research papers.*

A **compound sentence** *has two or more independent clauses but no dependent clauses. The clauses may be joined by a comma and a coordinating conjunction, or by a semicolon. Examples of coordinating conjunctions are* **for**, **and**, **nor**, **but**, **or**.

Example: *Sadie and Amia waited for the train,* **but** *the train was very late.*

A **complex sentence** *has one independent clause and one or more dependent clauses. Many dependent clauses are introduced by a subordinating conjunction. Examples of subordinating conjunctions are* **after, although, as, as soon as, because, before, even though, if, since, than, though, unless, until, when, whenever, wherever, which, while**.

Example: While Sadie and Amia waited at the train station, they realized the train was late.

        (dependent clause)   *(independent clause)*

A *sentence can also be both* **compound and complex**.

Identify each sentence below by writing **S** for simple, **CD** for compound, **CX** for complex, and **CD-CX** for compound-complex.

1. My grandmother, who is 84 years old, owns a condo near Myrtle Beach. _____

2. The magazine article was both timely and interesting. _____

3. My father must have lost the tickets, for they are not on the car seat. _____

4. Although we just purchased it, the cake is stale. _____

5. CDs and clothes were scattered all over Jake's room. _____

6. The ice skater performed a back flip, and the crowd rose to its feet. _____

7. Because the switch does not work, you need to buy a new flashlight. _____

8. Although I like to swim, I have neither had the time to go lately, nor have I found anyone to go with me. _____

Math Puzzles and Tricks

Solve the following math puzzles and tricks.

1. **On June 9 of this year, Walt Disney Studio created Donald Duck. To find the year:**
   • The tens and unit digits are consecutive integers whose sum is 7 and product is 12.
   • The tens digit is $\frac{1}{3}$ of the hundreds digit.
   • The sum of all the digits is 17.

   Donald Duck was created in _____ (year).

2. **To do this trick, you will need a calculator.**
   • First, enter the number 37037.
   • Next, multiply your favorite digit from 1 to 9 by 3 (Do this step in your head.)
   • Then, multiply the number in the calculator by the above answer (the number in your head).
   • Finally, you should end with a row of 6 of your favorite numbers.

   What is it? _____

3. **Astronaut Neil Armstrong became the first person to step on the moon. His famous quote is "That's one small step for a man, one giant leap for mankind." To find the year:**
   • The tens digit is a perfect number.
   • The hundreds and units digits are the same square number.
   • The sum of all the digits is 25.

   Neil Armstrong walked on the moon in _____.

4. **A two-hundred pound man and his two sons, each of whom weigh one hundred pounds, want to cross a river. They have only one boat that can only carry two hundred pounds.**

   How will they all cross the river? _____

   _____

   _____

5. **Write your house number, double it, add 5, multiply by 50, add your age, add 365, subtract 615. The answer will contain both your house number and your age.**

   _____

6. **You are the pilot of an airplane that flies from New York to Chicago, a distance of 1,000 miles. The plane's air speed averages 200 miles per hour and makes one 30 minute stop.**

   What is the pilot's name? _____

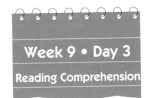

Alberto Santos Dumont: Brazil's Favorite Aviator

Most people have heard of the Wright Brothers, the two Americans generally considered the inventors of the first practical airplane. Few people other than Brazilians (and certain aviation enthusiasts) have heard of Alberto Santos Dumont, another visionary in early aviation.

Santos Dumont was born in 1873 in Minas Gerais, Brazil. When he turned 18, he was sent to Paris to study chemistry, astronomy, physics, and mechanics. He became interested in **dirigibles**, or airships held up by a "lighter-than-air" gas often contained in a balloon.

Santos Dumont's balloons won many races and prizes, including one in 1901 for circling the Eiffel Tower in less than 30 minutes. Reportedly, Santos Dumont took the 100,000 franc prize and split it among his workers and Paris's beggars.

After conquering the skies in lighter-than-air vehicles, Santos Dumont became interested in heavier-than-air vehicles. His *14-BIS* plane left the ground on November 12, 1906, to fly at a speed of approximately 37 km/h and a height of 6 meters to reach a total distance of 220 meters. This flight won him the Archdeacon Prize and demonstrated that a heavier-than-air vehicle could take off by its own means.

The Wright Brothers had flown their *Flyer I* in 1903 with the help of a catapult's launch. The Wright Flyer, once airborne, flew for longer distances at a higher altitude than the *14-BIS*. Therefore, most people consider the Wright Flyer the first practical airplane. Undaunted by this classification, Brazilians still celebrate Santos Dumont as a national hero.

Answer the following questions.

1. **Alberto Santos Dumont was—**
   A. a Wright brother.
   B. the developer of the *Flyer I*.
   C. an aviator and inventor.
   D. never celebrated in his birth country.

2. **Aviation's Latin root is *avis*, which probably means—**
   A. brick.
   B. bird.
   C. Brazilian.
   D. winner.

3. **A synonym for aviator is most likely—**
   A. enthusiast.
   B. beggar.
   C. winner.
   D. pilot.

4. **What happened first?**
   A. the Wright Brothers flew *Flyer I*.
   B. Santos Dumont flew the *14-BIS*.
   C. Santos Dumont won 100,000 francs.
   D. Santos Dumont won the Archdeacon.

5. **The difference between a dirigible and an airplane is—**
   A. one is lighter-than-air and one is heavier-than-air.
   B. dirigibles are more popular today.
   C. airplanes were invented first.
   D. there is no difference.

6. **Because Santos Dumont won the race—**
   A. he received the 100,000 franc prize.
   B. he gave his proceeds to charity.
   C. he built the *14-BIS*.
   D. he is a Brazilian national hero.

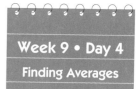
Mean, Mode, Median & Range

 Mean, median, and **mode** are three kinds of averages. **Range** is the difference between the largest and smallest value in the group of numbers.

1) To find the **mean** of a set of numbers, add all the numbers and then divide their sum by the number of addends.

2) The middle number in a set of numbers is the **median**. To find the **median**, the numbers must first be arranged in order. If there are two middle numbers (which will occur if there is an even number of addends), the **median** is the average of the two middle numbers.

3) **Mode** refers to the number that occurs most frequently in a set of numbers.

Find the mean, mode, median, and range for each data set.

1. Erik planted ten apple trees. He kept track of how many apples he picked from each tree. His results are shown in the table:

Tree #	1	2	3	4	5	6	7	8	9	10
# of Apples	137	120	140	141	137	124	119	129	137	136

Mean: _____ Median: _____ Mode: _____ Range: _____

2. Over the summer, Tamara read four mystery novels. The table shows how many pages each book had:

Book Title	An Eye for Mystery	Unbelievable!	The Treehouse Nextdoor	Treading Lightly
# of Pages	512	272	368	512

Mean: _____ Median: _____ Mode: _____ Range: _____

3. Seven friends have a contest to see how long they can balance their left foot. Their results are shown in the table:

Name	Adeela	Henry	Wendy	Kenny	Thea	Winston	Cyrus
Time (seconds)	56	35	88	65	91.6	35	63.4

Mean: _____ Median: _____ Mode: _____ Range: _____

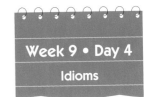

Warm-Up With Idioms

 Idioms *are the most difficult part of learning any language.* **Idioms** *are commonly used expressions that mean something different from the actual words. For example, "Clear as a bell" has nothing to do with bells ringing. The idiom means to be understood clearly.*

Underline the idiom in each sentence.

1. Jake and Maria almost missed their flight because it was down to the wire.

2. My sister was on top of the world when her team won the game.

3. It is time to face the music on your chocolate addiction.

4. If you choose to live high on the hog, you will spend all of your savings.

5. Break a leg in our school play today.

Match the idioms with their meanings.

_____ 6. blowing smoke   A. to talk about unimportant things

_____ 7. cold turkey   B. ability to grow flowers and plants

_____ 8. spill the beans   C. boasting without being able to back it up

_____ 9. chew the fat   D. give away a secret

_____ 10. green thumb   E. to quit something abruptly

Write sentences using each of the following idioms.

11. **in the doghouse** _____

12. **put your best foot forward** _____

13. **jump to conclusions** _____

14. **cut from the same cloth** _____

Planning a Story

A **narrative** tells a story. Answer the following questions to help plan your story.

What is the title?_____

Where will the story take place?_____

When will the story take place?_____

Who is the main character?_____

What is the main character like?_____

What problem or problems will your main character face?_____

_____

What other characters will you include?_____

What will be the most exciting moment or turning point?_____

_____

What events or actions will lead up to this moment?_____

_____

What events or actions will follow this moment and show how the problem is resolved?

_____

_____

What is the resolution?_____

Will you tell your story in the first-person or third-person point of view?_____

Now, review your plan. Make any revisions. Then write a draft of your story on another sheet
of paper. Begin by writing a topic sentence that will grab the attention of your reader.

Hidden Meters

Find three boxes horizontally, vertically, or diagonally whose sum is 1 meter. Pay close attention to whether the numbers are listed as mm, cm, dm, or m. There are 16 such trios. Ring each trio you see. You may use a calculator. One is done for you.

90 mm	11 cm	0.8 m	500 mm	40 cm	25 cm	0.5 m	0.25 m
200 mm	50 dm	60 cm	1 dm	30 cm	9 mm	1 cm	0.8 m
40 cm	1 cm	700 mm	8 cm	5 cm	4 dm	550 mm	50 cm
400 mm	0.3 m	300 mm	3 dm	40 cm	0.3 m	0.4 cm	300 cm
2 dm	3 dm	40 mm	15 mm	1.1 m	300 mm	9 m	0.5 m
0.3 cm	1 m	30 cm	600 mm	1 dm	8 dm	20 cm	350 mm
50 cm	0.45 m	1 dm	45 cm	2.5 cm	0.1 m	9 dm	15 cm
200 mm	3 dm	50 cm	0.95 m	4 cm	3 cm	0.80 m	40 dm
10 mm	250 mm	600 dm	4.5 dm	0.07 m	600 mm	70 cm	300 mm

Helping Your Middle Schooler Get Ready: Week 10

These are the skills your middle schoolers will be working on this week.

Math
- decimals
- algebra word problems

Reading
- reading for information

Writing
- sequencing
- personal narrative

Vocabulary
- word work: synonyms, antonyms, and idioms
- tricky words

Grammar
- adverbs
- future tense verbs

Here is an activity you and your middle schooler might enjoy.

Fun With Numbers Teach your middle schooler this number trick, and then he or she can amaze friends and family members. Tell your child you have a "magic" number. Write 61.74 on a slip of paper and fold it in half so your child can't see it. Then post the following steps, giving your child time to calculate each time. An example is given after each step.

1) Pick any four different numbers between 0 and 9. **(1, 5, 9, 6)**
2) Arrange them to make the greatest number possible. **(9651)**
3) Place a decimal between the two middle numbers. **(96.51)**
4) Then arrange them to make the least number possible. **(1569)**
5) Place a decimal between the two middle numbers. **(15.69)**
6) Subtract the second decimal number from the first.
(96.51 – 15.69 = 80.82)
7) Use the four numbers in the difference.
Repeat steps 2 through 6. **(88.20 – 02.88 = 85.32)**
8) Repeat the steps until arriving at the magic number.
(85.32 – 23.58 = 61.74)

Give the slip of paper to your child and ask him or her to open it. The number 61.74 will always appear sooner or later. It doesn't matter what numbers your child chooses.

Your middle schooler might enjoy reading one of the following books:

American Born Chinese
by Gene Luen Yang

Before Columbus: The Americas 1491
by Charles C. Mann

Heroes of the Environment: True Stories of People Who Are Helping to Protect Our Planet
by Harriet Rohmer

My Week at a Glance

Use this page to set goals and make journal entries.

Goals for Monday _____

_____

Journal: Would you rather have a week in the desert with temperatures over 100 degrees or a week on an iceberg? Explain.

_____

_____

_____

_____

Goals for Tuesday _____

Goals for Wednesday _____

_____

Journal: Would you rather live in a big city or a small town? Why?

_____

_____

_____

_____

Goals for Thursday _____

Goals for Friday _____

_____

Journal: A is for Angola; B is for Brazil. For how many letters of the alphabet can you name a country?

_____

_____

_____

_____

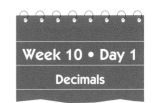
Stumpers

Write your answers in both number and word form; for example, 14.37 (number form), fourteen and thirty-seven hundredths (word form).

1. Who Am I?
A. I have 4 digits, and they all are different.
B. All of my digits are odd.
C. I have a 1 in the hundredths place.
D. I have a 7 in the ones place.
E. The number in the tens place is less than the number in the tenths place.
F. None of my digits is 9.

Answer: _____

_____

2. Who Am I?
A. I have 4 digits, and they are all odd.
B. The number in the tenths place is greater than 3. It is a factor of 36.
C. The number in the hundredths place is less than 4 and greater than 1.
D. The numbers in the ones and tens places are the same and are also factors of 25.

Answer: _____

_____

3. Who Am I?
A. I have 4 digits, and they are all different and even.
B. The number in the hundredths place is half of the number in the tenths place.
C. The number in the hundredths place is greater than 3.
D. The number in the ones place is 6.
E. The number in the tens place is 2.

Answer: _____

_____

4. Who Am I?
A. I have 4 digits.
B. Each digit is either a 2 or a 4.
C. The numbers in the ones place and tenths place are the same.
D. The numbers in the tens place and hundredths place are the same.
E. I have a 4 in the hundredths place.

Answer: _____

_____

5. Who Am I?
A. I have 3 even digits.
B. The number in the tenths place when subtracted from 3 equals 1.
C. The number in the ones place is 8.
D. Divide the number in the ones place by 2 and you will have the number in the hundredths place.

Answer: _____

_____

6. Who Am I?
A. I have 4 digits, and they are all odd.
B. The 2-digit whole number is greater than 10 and less than 20. When this number is divided into 121, the quotient is also that number.
C. The digit in the tenths place is 3.
D. Add 4 to the number in the tenths place and you will have the number in the hundredths place.

Answer: _____

_____

Adverbs That Compare

 *Adverbs can be used to compare actions. A **comparative adverb**, which compares two actions, ends in **-er** or begins with **more** or **less**. A **superlative adverb**, which compares more than two actions, ends in **-est** or begins with **most** or **least**. Adverbs that have more than one syllable or that end in –ly use the word **more** to form the comparative, and the word **most** to form the superlative.*

Comparative: *The sun is <u>closer</u> to Earth than any other star.*
We play soccer <u>more frequently</u> than baseball.

Superlative: *The sun is the <u>closest</u> star to Earth.*
Of all the sports to play, we play soccer <u>most frequently</u>.

Write in the blank the missing form of the adverb.

Adverb	Comparative	Superlative
1. fast	faster	_____
2. high	_____	highest
3. _____	sooner	soonest
4. carefully	_____	_____
5. long	_____	longest
6. _____	more regularly	_____
7. far	farther	_____

Underline the correct form of the adverb in parentheses.

8. Jonathan always eats (faster, fastest) than his brother does.

9. We go swimming (more often, oftener) now that the weather is warmer.

10. Carlos wins (more frequently, most frequently) than his brother Eduardo.

11. The owl can screech the (louder, loudest) of all the birds that I know.

12. Samantha will arrive (sooner, soonest) of the 12 guests.

13. Lauren sat (closer, closest) to the exit door than Debbie did.

14. Jennifer is studying (more long, longer) than usual because she has a test tomorrow.

15. Senator Roberts speaks the (intelligentliest, most intelligently) of all the candidates.

Pictures Are Worth a Thousand Words

Comic strips tell a story in a short sequence of sketches and possibly a few short captions or conversation bubbles. Think of the most exciting experience in your life so far. Write the story. Then break the story into sequential steps. You have six cells to tell your story. Remember: cell one sets the story, and cell six is the conclusion; therefore, you are left with four cells to give the highlights of the event. The artistic merit of the drawings is not as important as the clarity of the story you tell.

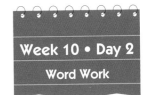

Vocabulary Review

This page reviews:

- **synonyms,** *words that have similar meanings.*
- **antonyms,** *words that have opposite meanings.*
- **idioms,** *expressions that have a figurative meaning that is different from what each individual word means.*

Underline the **synonym** for each boldface word in each row.

1. **flourish**	thrive	provide	feed
2. **conspicuous**	hidden	obvious	angry
3. **rescue**	stretch	jump	save
4. **drawback**	behind	disadvantage	artwork
5. **glisten**	sparkle	speak	hear

Underline the **antonym** of the boldface word in each row.

6. **advance**	retreat	forward	horizontal
7. **vertical**	straight	horizontal	advance
8. **placid**	feeble	calm	turbulent
9. **import**	export	empty	send
10. **inflate**	rise	import	deflate

Circle the letter of the correct meaning of each **idiom**.

11. **come to grips with**
    A. accept or deal with firmly
    B. shake hands firmly

12. **a far cry**
    A. calling to someone in a distance
    B. quite different; far removed

13. **on the dot**
    A. on the black spot
    B. exactly at the time agreed on; promptly

14. **showing your true colors**
    A. revealing your true nature
    B. exhibiting your paintings

Algebra Word Problems

Read these word problems carefully. Then, solve them using algebra. Show your work.

1. **Right now, Jamal's mother is 3 times older than Jamal. But in 12 years, her age will be exactly 2 times greater than Jamal's. How old are Jamal and his mother today?**

2. **Uncle Rupert asked Rachel to visit his farm to help count all the llamas and ostriches. The animals are running around really fast, but she's still sure she counted 35 heads and 94 feet. How many llamas are there? How many ostriches are there?**

3. **Larissa has a bag full of gumdrops. She knows there are fewer than 75 pieces of candy in all. When she divides them into groups of 3, 4, 5, or 6, there is always 1 gumdrop left over. How many gumdrops does Larissa have?**

4. **The sum of the ages of the three Perez sisters is 50. Rosa is the youngest, Elena is the middle sister, and Felicia is the oldest—10 years older than Rosa. Five years ago, their ages were prime numbers. How old was each then?**

5. **A pen and a pencil together cost $5.10. The pen costs $5 more than the pencil. How much does each cost?**

6. **In the basketball league Ivy belongs to, 2 points are awarded for every shot made and 3 points are deducted for every shot missed. In one game, Ivy took 40 shots but scored 0 points. How many shots did she make? How many did she miss?**

7. **Luisa noticed that in 7 years she'll be half her mother's age. If 3 years ago Luisa was $\frac{1}{3}$ her mother's age, how old is her mother now?**

8. **Kevin can do a job in 4 hours. It takes Kendra 2 hours to do the same job. If they do the job together, how long will it take them?**

Troublesome Verbs

 There are four verbs that often create problems for many writers: lay *and* lie, set *and* sit.

The verb lay *means* to place.
Examples: George, please <u>lay</u> the towels on the bathroom shelves. (present)
Joey <u>laid</u> the tile floor last week. (past)
Thomas <u>has laid</u> the two library books on the counter. (past participle)

The verb lie *means* to recline.
Examples: My baby sister <u>lies</u> in her crib until she awakes. (present)
As a child, I <u>lay</u> down for a nap every afternoon. (past)
The gifts <u>have lain</u> on the kitchen table since yesterday. (past participle)

Circle the best answer in the parentheses.

1. **The cat likes to (lay, lie) near the warm stove.**

2. **The tile installers have (laid, lain) the floor to the patio.**

3. **Please (lay, lie) your essay on the desk when you have finished.**

4. **(Lay, Lie) the plastic cups and plates on the picnic table.**

The verb sit *means* to be in a seat *or* to rest.
Examples: Kenny <u>sits</u> in the third row at the ball game. (present)
Kenny <u>sat</u> in the third row before (past)
Kenny <u>has sat</u> there in the third row often. (past participle)

The verb set *means* to put *or* place something.
Examples: Lauren <u>sets</u> the plates on the table every day. (present)
Lauren <u>set</u> the plates on the table yesterday. (past)
Lauren <u>has set</u> the plates on the table since she was a young girl. (past participle)

Circle the best answer in the parentheses.

5. **No one may (sit, set) on the patio while it is raining.**

6. **Please carefully (sit, set) the expensive vase on the dining room table.**

7. **Janie had (sat, set) the vase there many times.**

8. **Our next door neighbors (sit, sat) with us during the concert.**

The Art of Deception

A beautiful but poisonous lion fish glides past. Wait, or is it a sea snake? Or a flat sole fish slipping down across the sand? There is an animal that can look like all of these creatures, and more.

The mimic octopus was discovered in 1998 in a river in Indonesia. It grows to about two feet in length and normally is striped white and brown. However, as its common name suggests, the mimic octopus changes its shape, color, and behavior to **mimic**, or appear like, other animals. This adaptation has developed over time to help the animal protect itself from predators.

While some other octopuses **camouflage** themselves, changing their color to blend into their environment, the mimic octopus changes its color and behavior to resemble dangerous animals. This represents a risky strategy for the octopus; instead of remaining safely hidden it must actively swim out and hope that its performance is good enough to fool predators. This form of mimicry, where a harmless species mimics a dangerous species, is called **Batesian mimicry**.

What Makes the Mimic Octopus Special?

Although many animals use mimicry to survive, the mimic octopus is the first known species to mimic several different animals.

This talented octopus has three confirmed impersonations: the lion fish, the sea snake, and the sole fish. To impersonate a poisonous lion fish, it floats above the sea floor, spreading its arms wide to resemble the lion fish's fins. For a sea snake impersonation, the octopus' color shifts to the red and black bands associated with the venomous snake and wriggles two arms in different directions. To create the illusion of a toxic sole fish, it pulls its arms together into a heart shape, uses jet propulsion to build up speed, and undulates across the sea floor. The mimic octopus is also believed to take on the form of sand anemones, mantis shrimp, stingrays, and jellyfish.

Another remarkable attribute of the mimic octopus is that it seems to know which creature to impersonate to scare off its current predator. This demonstrates the octopus's high intelligence. For instance, when a mimic octopus is attacked by a damselfish, it imitates a banded sea snake, one of the damselfish's known predators. By taking on the appearance of a known predator of its attacker, the octopus is more likely to scare off its attacker.

A Recent Discovery

Researchers had not previously discovered the mimic octopus because its habitat is not a very popular place for divers to explore. The muddy river bottom lacks the vibrant diversity of life available in areas like the coral reefs. However, the stark nature of the landscape may have prompted the mimic octopus' unusual adaptation. Since there is nowhere to hide, the octopus must either retreat into the ground or pretend to be something else. Scientists speculate that there may be even more species of mimic octopuses left to discover in more murky river bottoms.

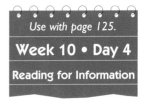
Answer the following questions that relate to the preceding passage.

1. **Someone that mimics—**
   A. eats something that looks like itself.
   B. looks, acts, or sounds like someone or something else.
   C. cannot blend in to their environment.
   D. is afraid of mimes.

2. **The mimic octopus lives—**
   A. in forests near orb weaver spiders.
   B. in the coral reefs in Australia.
   C. in murky river bottoms in Indonesia.
   D. at the bottom of the Pacific Ocean.

3. **The antonym of camouflage is—**
   A. reveal.
   B. hide.
   C. army.
   D. civilian.

4. **When not mimicking, the mimic octopus—**
   A. hisses like a snake.
   B. turns completely black.
   C. has white and brown stripes.
   D. undulates like a sole fish.

5. **Batesian mimicry is demonstrated when—**
   A. a harmless species mimics a harmful one.
   B. two harmful species mimic each other.
   C. a creature hides itself in the sand.
   D. someone named Bates mimics you.

6. **Another title for this story could be—**
   A. Orb Weaver Spiders and Other Mimics.
   B. New Octopus Discovered in 1998.
   C. The Mimic Octopus: Nature's Best Performer.
   D. A Damselfish Attacks: A Sea Floor Survival Guide.

7. **When a damselfish appears, a mimic octopus will usually—**
   A. imitate a flat sole fish.
   B. imitate a banded sea snake.
   C. camouflage itself among the sand.
   D. run and hide.

8. **The mimic octopus's behavior in Question 7 demonstrates—**
   A. the octopus's high level of intelligence.
   B. a form of Batesian mimicry.
   C. both A and B.
   D. none of the above.

9. **Three animals the mimic octopus imitates are—**
   A. the lion fish, sea snake, and sole fish.
   B. the lion fish, dormouse, and sole fish.
   C. are the lion fish, damsel fish, and orb weaver spider.
   D. are the lion fish, jellyfish, and Monarch.

10. **The mimic octopus's habitat is—**
    A. filled with verdant colors.
    B. the coral reefs.
    C. popular with scuba divers.
    D. murky river bottoms.

11. **The mimic octopus was only discovered in 1998 because—**
    A. the coral reefs are heavily protected.
    B. it lives in a popular area for divers.
    C. it lives in an unpopular area for divers.
    D. it is so good at mimicry.

12. **Extending the previous answer, the most likely place to discover new creatures is—**
    A. in coral reefs.
    B. in popular areas.
    C. in unpopular areas.
    D. in areas with much mimicry.

For the Future

Future tense verbs *tell about action that hasn't happened yet. Use* **will** *with a verb to show future tense.*

Complete this poster for the Totally Terrific Talent Show. Use a different verb to tell what talent each performer will share.

Totally Terrific Talent Show

1. Mister Greene _____ your host for the evening.

2. To open the show, the Tempo Trio _____ the "Star-Spangled Banner."

3. Next on the bill, Kiyoko Sato _____ her experimental blend of ballet and hip-hop.

4. Gilbert Lopez _____ a classical guitar interlude.

5. Scoot up to the edge of your seat! The Amazing Sabarisi _____ jaw-dropping magic tricks.

6. College roommates Bronwyn and Jessica _____ original poetry.

7. So everyone leaves in a good mood, Freddy Funniman _____ the most hilarious jokes in his repertoire!

8. You _____ the best time in your life!

127

"Gr.8" Expectations

As the summer winds down and the new school year approaches, it is an excellent time to think about eighth grade expectations. Write a letter to yourself about what you hope to accomplish during the upcoming school year.

Be sure to think about social, athletic, maturational, and life goals as well as strictly academic ones.

_____,

_____

_____

_____

_____

_____

_____

_____

_____

_____

_____

_____

Answer Key

Week 1

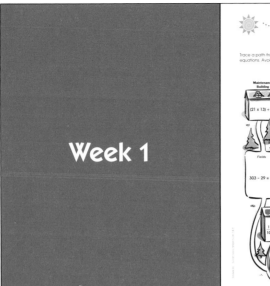

page 11

Lost at Camp

Trace a path from the Parking Lot to the Campfire Circle by following eight correctly written equations. Avoid ones with mistakes.

page 12

It's Only Proper!

A **common noun** names any person, place, thing, or idea. A **proper noun** names a particular person, place, thing, or idea. Here are some examples of common and proper nouns. Common nouns are not capitalized, but proper nouns are.

Common Nouns	Proper Nouns
city	Atlanta
river	Mississippi River
poet	Maya Angelou
street	Main Street
organization	Boy Scouts of America

Read the following sentences. Underline the common nouns and circle the proper nouns.

1. Monaco is the second smallest country in Europe.
2. Brittany and her two best friends live on Washington Street.
3. The American Red Cross brings aid to people during disasters.
4. The United States is a democratic country.
5. William Butler Yeats wrote beautiful poetry!
6. He wrote the poem, "The Lake Isle of Innisfree."
7. This Irish land must be quite special to the poet.
8. The place of which Yeats wrote is near Sligo, Ireland.
9. The sights beyond the lake include views of the Lough Gill Mountains.
10. The Hazelwood Sculpture Trail is close to the lake.
11. The United Nations is in New York City.
12. Nathan is an excellent guitarist.
13. Australia is the smallest continent.
14. Lincoln Avenue is our town's busiest street.
15. Josh and Molly are cousins.

page 13

Hatshepsut

Throughout the long history of Ancient Egypt, its rulers, or **pharaohs**, were almost always men. But one woman did succeed in becoming pharaoh. Hatshepsut was a princess married to a pharaoh. When her husband died, her 10-year-old stepson should have become the pharaoh. But Hatshepsut saw a chance to seize power. She claimed the boy was too young to rule and demanded to be named his co-ruler.

To be sure people saw her as pharaoh, Hatshepsut had to dress the part. She adopted all of the **accoutrements** of a pharaoh: the headdress, clothes, and even the fake beard worn by all of Egypt's pharaohs.

Hatshepsut not only looked the part of a powerful leader, she acted it. Historians characterize her reign as a time of peace and prosperity for Egypt. She oversaw the creation of many great works of art, restored religious temples, and, most important, organized trade networks. She ruled Egypt for 20 years.

After her death, Hatshepsut's stepson, Thuthmose III, came to power. Unfortunately, he attempted to erase Hatshepsut from history. He began destroying everything he could find with her image or name on it. Despite Thuthmose III's efforts, some artifacts remained for researchers to unearth. Archaeologists found evidence of Hatshepsut's rule, and today we know many things about this successful female pharaoh.

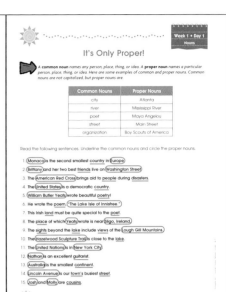

Answer the following questions.

1. Hatshepsut was—
   A. an archaeologist.
   B. a pharaoh.
   C. an Egyptian model.
   D. a historian.

2. A pharaoh is—
   A. always male.
   B. an archaeologist.
   C. the name for a ruler of Ancient Egypt.
   D. a princess.

3. What happened first?
   A. Hatshepsut restored temples.
   B. Thuthmose III came to power.
   C. Researchers uncovered her story.
   D. Hatshepsut became pharaoh.

4. Hatshepsut's reign is characterized by—
   A. peace and prosperity.
   B. uprisings against the throne.
   C. destruction of Thuthmose III's image.
   D. unrelenting drought and famine.

5. Accoutrements refer to—
   A. great works of art.
   B. a successor to the throne.
   C. clothing and accessories.
   D. acts of royal vandalism.

6. When Thuthmose III claimed the throne—
   A. an age of peace and prosperity began.
   B. he tried to erase any sign of Hatshepsut.
   C. he became the first female pharaoh.
   D. he decided not to wear a false beard.

7. Hatshepsut's story was discovered by—
   A. researchers.
   B. a pharaoh.
   C. Thuthmose III.
   D. her husband.

8. To look like a pharaoh, Hatshepsut—
   A. learned a sacred dance.
   B. studied in Greece under philosophers.
   C. decided to retire after 20 years.
   D. wore special clothes and a fake beard.

page 14

Vocabulary Building: Context Clues

You can sometimes find the meaning of an unfamiliar word by using context clues, or the words or phrases around the word.

Using context clues, underline the correct word to complete each sentence.

1. The sad news made Malik feel very (somber, elated).
2. During a hectic day, reading a book is a welcome (interlude, intermediate) for Carmen.
3. Because of her (persistence, resistance), Leticia finally learned to drive a car.
4. Janie loves vegetables more than anything, so she (avoids, prefers) cheeseburgers.
5. Mario improved his (endurance, resistance) during swim meets by practicing every day.
6. Jonathan's track team drank gallons of lemonade after their track meet because they were so (dehydrated, depopulated).

Complete each sentence below by choosing a word from the word box that makes sense in the blank. Be sure to use the context clues in the sentence to help you.

erode	aerospace	hydrant	manipulate	participate

1. In case of fire at your house, would you be able to direct the fire department to the nearest hydrant?
2. An airplane pilot has to manipulate the controls in order to fly the plane.
3. Wind and running water continually erode, or wear away, soil and rocks.
4. Eliot cannot participate in sports after school because he must go home to take care of his brother.
5. Because Yoko is planning an aerospace career, she is studying about the earth's atmosphere.

page 15

A Graph Puzzle

Use the graph on the next page. Follow the directions to complete this puzzle.

1. Plot each ordered pair below, and then connect all the points with a straight line segment.

(4, 1)	(-10, 7)	$(-7\frac{1}{2}, -3)$
(8, 0)	$(-9\frac{1}{2}, 8\frac{1}{2})$	(-6, -1)
(14, 3)	(-14, 6)	(-4, -1)
(20, 10)	$(-15, 4\frac{1}{2})$	(-6, -7)
(9, 4)	$(-16, 1\frac{1}{2})$	$(-12\frac{1}{2}, -11)$
(6, 4)	(-15, 0)	(-11, -11)
(2, 7)	$(-13\frac{1}{2}, 2)$	(-5, -9)
(-2, 8)	(-8, -1)	(1, -3)
(-6, 7)	(-7, -1)	(4, 1)
(-10, 4)	$(-8\frac{1}{2}, -3)$	Plot this ordered pair. Do not connect.
(-13, 6)	(-7, -4)	(-14, 4)

page 16

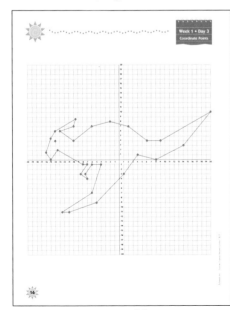

page 17

Dependent and Independent Clauses

A **clause** is a group of related words. A clause has both a subject and a predicate. There are two types of clauses, independent and dependent.

Independent Clause—An independent clause can stand alone as a sentence.
Example: We walked to the park last night.
Dependent Clause—A dependent clause cannot stand alone as a sentence.
Example: When we checked the cookies in the oven.

Read each clause. Write **I** for an independent clause. Write **D** for a dependent clause.

D   1. Because you enjoy pizza so much.
D   2. After you have finished the yard work.
I   3. The library book that you want is on the third shelf.
D   4. Although she enjoys playing the piano.
I   5. There must be a way to solve this problem.
I   6. I am too busy to go to the movies tonight.
D   7. Since they left here to go to San Francisco.
I   8. Eduardo waved to his friends.

Read each sentence. Circle each independent clause and underline each dependent clause.

9. As the population increases, the world faces a shortage of fresh water.
10. We ordered spaghetti, which everyone in the family likes.
11. While my brothers were working during the summer, I went to summer school.
12. Please show me the book that you read this summer.

page 18

Money Saving Coupons

Read each coupon. Then, solve the word problems.

1. The dance team is having a sleepover Friday evening before the team's car washing fundraiser. Meredith found a donut special at Dizzy Donuts for $4.60 per dozen. She purchased six dozen donuts. Her total bill for the donuts was
   $ 27.60

Dizzy Donuts Special
$4.60 for a Dozen Donuts
Good Anytime—Limit 6 Dozen

2. Best Ever chocolate chip cookies are $3.79 per bag at the Super Special Market. Super Special doubles the value of coupons on Tuesdays. Sue is shopping on Tuesday and buys two packages of cookies. What is the cost of cookies, not including taxes?
   $ 6.08

Save 75¢ on 2 Packages of Best Ever Chocolate Chip Cookies
No Expiration Date

3. Hotter Than Hot costs $1.79 per bottle. On a triple-value coupon day, what would be the cost before taxes per bottle?
   $ 1.04

Hotter Than Hot Pepper Sauce
Save 25¢ per Bottle
Good until September 1

4. The Testa family had lunch at Osvaldo's. Each of the four family members had three tacos at a cost of $2.50 each. Mr. and Mrs. Testa each had iced tea for $1.95, and the girls each had a soft drink for the same price. What was their check before taxes and tip, but after the discount? Read the coupon carefully!
   $ 30.24

Osvaldo's Outrageous Tacos
Present this coupon for 20% OFF entire food purchase
Good thru August 31

5. John's Car Care Center normally charges $39.95 for the special oil change. According to the coupon, what will the discounted price be? (Round to the nearest penny.)
   $ 33.96

John's Car Care Center
15% Discount on Oil Change with this coupon
Expires October 31

page 19

Descriptive Writing Prompt

Think about the last time you attended a special event, such as a baseball game, a concert, a trip to an amusement park, or a field trip. Follow the steps below to write a descriptive paragraph about the event.

1. Select a topic for your special event:

2. Use this graphic organizer to brainstorm ways to describe the event using your five senses.

EVENT

see   smell   hear   touch   taste

3. Make an outline, using your ideas from above. Include descriptions related to at least three senses and two supporting details for each point.

Title

I.
  A.
  B.
  C.
II.
  A.
  B.
  C.
III.
  A.
  B.

Answers will vary.

page 20

Descriptive Writing

Next, write a draft on a separate sheet of paper based on the outline that you created. Edit the first draft and recopy your final paragraph on the lines below. Be sure to share your paragraph with your family.

Title

Answers will vary.

Week 2

page 23

What a Combination!

Short sentences can sometimes make writing sound choppy. By combining sentences, you can help make your writing read more smoothly.

Example: My best friend loves to go horseback riding. I love to go horseback riding.
My best friend and I love to go horseback riding.

Read each pair of sentences below. Then combine the sentences into one sentence. Write the new sentence on the lines.

Answers will vary but should resemble these examples.

1. My mom made my favorite dessert. She made pecan pie.
My mom made my favorite dessert, pecan pie.

2. On vacation we went swimming every day. We collected shells on the beach every day.
On vacation, we went swimming and collected shells on the beach every day.

3. Beethoven was a brilliant composer. He eventually lost his hearing.
Beethoven was a brilliant composer who eventually lost his hearing.

4. Charles Dickens wrote *A Tale of Two Cities*. Charles Dickens is my favorite writer.
Charles Dickens, who wrote *A Tale of Two Cities*, is my favorite writer.

5. Ants are tiny creatures of great strength. Ants can lift ten times their own weight.
Ants are tiny creatures of great strength that can lift ten times their own weight.

6. Carmen can jump higher than anyone else on the track team. She can also jump farther than anyone on the team.
Carmen can jump higher and farther than anyone else on the track team.

7. One of my best friends is Matt Johnson. He is a great baseball player.
Matt Johnson is a great baseball player and one of my best friends.

8. My family's pet is an all-white cat. She is named Snowball.
My family's pet is an all-white cat named Snowball.

9. The car wash was closed yesterday. The bank was closed, too.
The car wash and bank were closed yesterday.

10. The parade will have marching bands. The parade will have colorful floats.
The parade will have marching bands and colorful floats.

page 24

Fraction Action

Solve the problems. Be sure you check the signs. Give your answers in the lowest terms.

1. $\frac{4}{7} + \frac{6}{11} = 1\frac{9}{77}$

5. $\frac{6}{9} + \frac{9}{18} = 2\frac{1}{18}$

9. $3\frac{7}{9} + 4\frac{4}{9} = 8\frac{2}{9}$

13. $2\frac{3}{4} + 3\frac{4}{5} = 6\frac{11}{20}$

2. $\frac{4}{5} - \frac{3}{5} - \frac{1}{5} = 0$

6. $\frac{2}{5} - \frac{1}{3} = \frac{1}{15}$

10. $4\frac{1}{3} - 1\frac{2}{5} = 2\frac{14}{15}$

14. $4\frac{1}{4} - 1\frac{5}{6} = 2\frac{5}{12}$

3. $2 \cdot \frac{1}{4} = \frac{1}{2}$

7. $\frac{2}{3} \cdot \frac{2}{3} = \frac{4}{9}$

11. $3\frac{3}{4} \cdot 2 = 7\frac{1}{2}$

15. $3\frac{1}{7} \cdot 1\frac{3}{4} = 5\frac{1}{2}$

4. $3 \div \frac{1}{4} = 12$

8. $\frac{1}{2} \div \frac{4}{5} = \frac{5}{8}$

12. $6 \div 3\frac{1}{2} = 1\frac{7}{11}$

16. $1\frac{1}{5} \cdot 2\frac{1}{6} = \frac{36}{65}$

page 25

Capitalization & Punctuation

Read each group of sentences. Circle the one sentence that shows correct capitalization and punctuation.

1. A. Jessica called, and wants to know if you saw life as we know it.
   B. The movie was good, but the ticket price was too high.
   C. My friends and I, go to the Movies about once a week.
   D. We pay for our movie tickets, by working on Saturday.

2. A. Ronda wondered, "where does the foil come from to make the experiment?"
   B. "The foil is always here when we start the experiment said Tommy.
   C. "Before we arrive," Emily added, "Mr. Daily sets up the lab."
   D. "I think you are right," said Audrey

3. A. A computer and monitor will cost about one thousand dollars.
   B. The desk that you ordered, will arrive next Monday.
   C. When the desk and computer are delivered, my brother, and I will help.
   D. How much should I pay for delivery.

4. A. Rachel was born on October 10 1997.
   B. Rachel was born on October 10, 1997.
   C. Rachel was born on October 10. 1997.
   D. Rachel was born on October 10, 1997.

5. A. Marcia asked, "Will you be going to the party with us tomorrow, Julie?"
   B. Marcia asked, "Will you be going to the party with us tomorrow Julie?"
   C. Marcia asked, "Will you be going to the party with us tomorrow, Julie."
   D. Marcia asked, "Will you be going to the party with us tomorrow, Julie?"

6. A. "Stop thief!" she screamed
   B. "Stop thief!" she screamed.
   C. "Stop thief!" she screamed.
   D. "Stop thief," she screamed.

7. A. My friend Marcus, who is an artist displays his works at the small corner gallery downtown.
   B. Before the movie began, we had to sit through many boring commercials?
   C. My mother's job is quite demanding; however, she is on time every day.
   D. Do you know where we are, Thomas?

8. A. Our plane will arrive in Boston by 11 o'clock because the pilot took a shortcut.
   B. Besides Elvis Presley, who has had the most influence on rock music?
   C. My sister always asks, "When will I get my driver's license?"
   D. All the above sentences are correct.

9. A. Peter can speak English Chinese, French and Japanese.
   B. Juan enjoys playing soccer but Oscar prefers playing field hockey
   C. Have you read John steinbecks book *Travels with Charley?*
   D. All the above sentences are incorrect.

10. A. We visited Utah, Idaho, and Wyoming.
    B. We visited Utah Idaho, and Wyoming.
    C. We visited Utah, Idaho and Wyoming.
    D. We visited Utah Idaho and Wyoming.

page 26

Order, Please!

Read each set of words below. Place the words in order as directed. Then compare your choices with a friend or family member to see if they agree.

1. (slow → fast)
trot, creep, dash, amble, jog
creep, amble, trot, jog, dash

2. (small → large)
tiny, bulky, infinitesimal, gargantuan, intermediate
infinitesimal, tiny, intermediate, bulky, gargantuan

3. (ugly → beautiful)
hideous, stunning, unsightly, attractive, pleasant
hideous, unsightly, pleasant, attractive, stunning

4. (soft → loud)
state, whisper, bark, bellow, shout
whisper, state, bark, shout, bellow

5. (boring → exciting)
bland, interesting, motivating, exhilarating, mind-numbing
mind-numbing, bland, interesting, motivating, exhilarating

6. (weak → strong)
delicate, sturdy, robust, omnipotent, sound
delicate, sound, sturdy, robust, omnipotent

7. (dark → bright)
dazzling, gloomy, jet-black, shady, luminous
jet-black, gloomy, shady, dazzling, luminous

8. (sad → happy)
blissful, despondent, content, downcast, ecstatic
despondent, downcast, content, blissful, ecstatic

Possible answers. Accept reasonable choices.

page 27

Order of Operations Review

The mnemonic, *Please Excuse My Dear Aunt Sally*, is a great way to remember the order of operations in a math problem. Here's how it works:

Please is for parentheses.   First, calculate inside the parentheses.
Excuse is for exponents.   Second, find the value of terms with exponents.
My Dear is for multiplication or division.   Third, multiply or divide.
Aunt Sally is for addition or subtraction.   Last, add or subtract.

Example: $3^2 \times (4 + 3) + 6 \div 3$
1) Work inside parentheses first. $3^2 \times (4+3) + 6 \div 3$
2) Next, simplify any terms with exponents. $3^2 \times 7 + 6 \div 3$
3) Multiply and divide from left to right. $9 \times 7 + 6 \div 3$
4) Add and subtract from left to right. $63 + 2$
                                          65

Evaluate each of the following expressions.

1. $(8 - 2) \cdot 2 \cdot 2 = 24$
2. $(13 - 32) \cdot 4 = -76$
3. $(27 \div 32) \cdot 7 = 5.9$
4. $(9 + 6) \div 3 = 5$
5. $(8 - 1) \cdot 4 + 3 = 31$
6. $22 \cdot 10 \div 5 + 3 = 47$
7. $(17 - 10) - 7 = 0$
8. $9 + 42 - 2 = 49$
9. $10 - 22 \cdot 2 = -34$
10. $52 \cdot 3 + 2 = 58$

11. $(5 + 2) \cdot (4 + 3) = 49$
12. $76 - 7 \cdot 22 = -78$
13. $2 \cdot (3 + 5) - 7 = 9$
14. $24 - 22 \cdot 3 = -42$
15. $(62 - 3) + 5 = 64$
16. $6 [(9 + 5) - 2 (3)] = 48$
17. $(8 - 1) \cdot 4 + 3 = 31$
18. $4 + (22 - 3) + 5 = 28$
19. $2 (6 (9 + 5) - 2 (3)) = 156$
20. $(52 - 5) \cdot 5 + 25 = 9.4$

Challenge: What combination of operations would make the following statement true?

$(15 \underline{-} 3) \underline{X} 17 \underline{+} 1 = 205$

page 28

An Albatross Around Your Neck

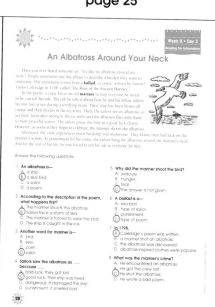

Have you ever heard someone say, "It's like an albatross around my neck"? People sometimes use this phrase to describe a burden they want to overcome. The expression comes from a **ballad**, or poem, written by Samuel Taylor Coleridge in 1798, called "The Rime of the Ancient Mariner."

In the poem, a curse forces an old **mariner** to stop everyone he meets so he can tell his tale. The tale he tells is about how he and his fellow sailors became lost at sea during a terrifying storm. Their ship has been blown off course and then freezes in the icy water. Then, the sailors see an albatross, or sea bird. Soon after seeing it, the ice melts and the albatross flies with them to more peaceful waters. The sailors praise the bird as a good luck charm. However, as soon as they begin to celebrate, the mariner shoots the albatross.

Afterward, the crew experiences much hardship and misfortune. They blame their bad luck on the mariner's action. As punishment for his crime, the sailors hang the albatross around the mariner's neck. And for the rest of his life, he was forced to tell his tale to everyone he met.

Answer the following questions.

1. An albatross is—
   A. a ship.
   B. a sea bird.
   C. a sailor.
   D. a poem.

2. According to the description of the poem, what happens first?
   A. The mariner shoots the albatross.
   B. Sailors face a storm at sea.
   C. The mariner is forced to wear the bird.
   D. The ship is caught in the ice.

3. Another word for *mariner* is—
   A. bird.
   B. sea.
   C. poet.
   D. sailor.

4. Sailors saw the albatross as because
   A. bad luck, their ship got lost.
   B. good luck, their ship was freed.
   C. dangerous, it damaged the ship.
   D. punishment, it smelled bad.

5. Why did the mariner shoot the bird?
   A. jealousy.
   B. hunger.
   C. fear.
   D. the answer is not given.

6. A *ballad* is a—
   A. sea bird.
   B. type of sailor.
   C. punishment.
   D. type of poem.

7. In 1798,
   A. Coleridge's poem was written.
   B. a mariner shot an albatross.
   C. the albatross was discovered.
   D. albatross-inspired clothes were popular.

8. What was the mariner's crime?
   A. He encountered an albatross.
   B. He shot the mariner.
   C. He shot the albatross.
   D. He wrote a bad poem.

Expository or Informational Essays

Many standardized tests ask students to write an essay in response to a prompt. Students are often given a few prompts to choose from. Write some notes about each prompt below. Then use your notes to choose a prompt for an essay. Write your essay on a separate sheet of paper.

Prompt 1
Write some notes explaining why someone you care about is important to you.

Answers will vary.

Prompt 2
Write some notes explaining how you have changed since you entered middle school.

Answers will vary.

Prompt 3
Write some notes explaining the importance of honesty in a friendship.

Answers will vary.

29

"Big Wind"

When several thunderstorms spiral together and grow into one giant storm, it is no longer a thunderstorm—it's a hurricane. Officially, scientists consider a storm a hurricane once its winds reach 74 mph (miles per hour). The word hurricane comes from the Taino Indian word urican, meaning "big wind." In the Atlantic Ocean, hurricanes only start in the tropics—the area five degrees north or south of the equator. If a large area of water in this part of the ocean is at least 80° F, and wind is blowing westward from Africa, conditions are just right for a hurricane. The warm, moist air of the ocean rises. As it rises, it cools, causing the water vapor to condense and form cumulonimbus clouds. As the cloud column grows larger and higher, it creates a circular pattern of wind. As the winds circle faster and faster, they twist around a calm center, called the eye. Once hurricanes hit land, they weaken because warm ocean water is no longer available to help them grow. But before they weaken, these fierce storms can cause severe damage.

Read each of the following questions and write the letter for the best answer on the line provided.

C 1. For a hurricane to form in the Atlantic Ocean, the water temperature must be—
A. less than 80° F. C. at least 80° F.
B. 74 mph. D. 5 degrees.

B 2. At what wind speed do scientists classify thunderstorms as hurricanes?
A. 30 mph C. 80 mph
B. 74 mph D. 50 mph

C 3. The calm center of a hurricane is called the—
A. vapor. C. eye.
B. tropics. D. urican.

A 4. Hurricanes weaken when—
A. they hit land. C. wind blows from Africa.
B. they form cumulonimbus clouds. D. warm, moist air rises.

Decide if the following statements are True (T) or False (F). Write your choice on the line provided.

T 1. Hurricane comes from the Taino Indian word urican.

T 2. The tropics is an area five degrees north and five degrees south of the equator.

F 3. Cumulonimbus clouds cause hurricanes.

F 4. The eye of the hurricane has the strongest winds.

30

Tangrams, "The Broken Squares"

A tangram consists of a square divided into seven geometric shapes: two large triangles, one medium triangle, two small triangles, one square, and one parallelogram. These pieces can be arranged into many geometric shapes and "pictures." Tangrams are one of the oldest geometric puzzles in the world.

Here's a story often told about how tangrams came to be. About 4,000 years ago in China, a man named Tan was on his way to show the emperor his treasured tile. But the tile fell to the floor and broke into seven pieces. For the rest of his life, Tan entertained himself and his friends with his "pictures" created from these seven pieces. He first used the tile pieces to make a picture of his cat and the pagoda where he often meditated. Tan's puzzle has been passed from generation to generation and country to country. It is said that more than three hundred designs hide within the "broken square."

Directions for folding and cutting a tangram.

Step 1—Cut a four-inch by four-inch square out of heavy paper; the front of a cereal box works well.

Step 2—Draw a diagonal that divides the square into two congruent triangles. Cut along the line to separate.

Step 3—Fold one of the two congruent triangles into two smaller congruent triangles. Cut along the fold to separate.

Step 4—Take the other large triangle and fold the top point (vertice A) to the midpoint of line segment BC. Then cut along the fold to create the middle-sized triangle and a trapezoid.

Step 5—Fold the trapezoid in half as shown in the diagram so that endpoints B and C meet. Cut in half at the fold to create two trapezoids.

Step 6—Cut one trapezoid into a triangle and quadrilateral.

Step 7—Cut the other trapezoid into a square and triangle.

Step 8—Now you should have 2 large triangles, 1 medium triangle, 2 small triangles, 1 square, and 1 parallelogram.

31

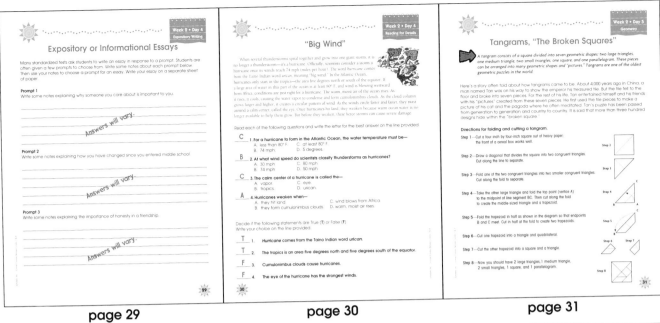

Solving Tangram Problems

Now that you have created your tangram, use the pieces to solve the following puzzles. The number in the center of the design represents the number of tangram pieces in the puzzle.

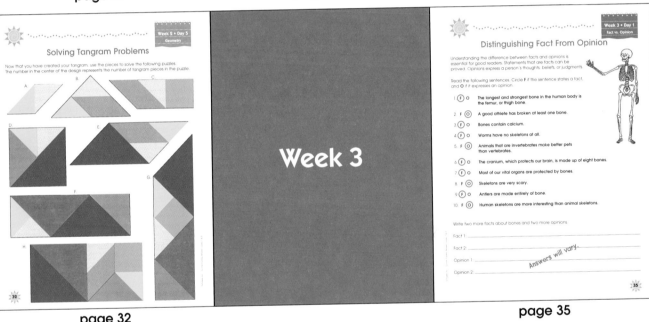

32

Week 3

Distinguishing Fact From Opinion

Understanding the difference between facts and opinions is essential for good readers. Statements that are facts can be proved. Opinions express a person's thoughts, beliefs, or judgments.

Read the following sentences. Circle **F** if the sentence states a fact, and **O** if it expresses an opinion.

1. **F** O The longest and strongest bone in the human body is the femur, or thigh bone.
2. F **O** A good athlete has broken at least one bone.
3. **F** O Bones contain calcium.
4. **F** O Worms have no skeletons at all.
5. F **O** Animals that are invertebrates make better pets than vertebrates.
6. **F** O The cranium, which protects our brain, is made up of eight bones.
7. **F** O Most of our vital organs are protected by bones.
8. F **O** Skeletons are very scary.
9. **F** O Antlers are made entirely of bone.
10. F **O** Human skeletons are more interesting than animal skeletons.

Write two more facts about bones and two more opinions.

Fact 1:
Fact 2:
Opinion 1:
Opinion 2:

Answers will vary.

35

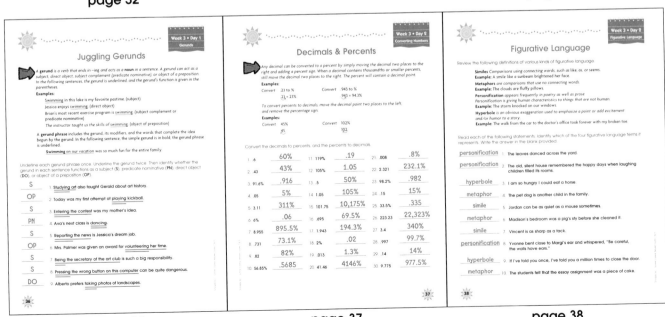

Juggling Gerunds

A gerund is a verb that ends in –ing and acts as a noun in a sentence. A gerund can act as a subject, direct object, subject complement (predicate nominative), or object of a preposition. In the following sentences, each example of the gerund is underlined, and the gerund's function is given in the parentheses.

Examples:
Swimming in this lake is my favorite pastime. (subject)
Jessica enjoys swimming. (direct object)
Brian's most recent exercise program is swimming. (subject complement or predicate nominative)
The instructor taught us the skills of swimming. (object of preposition)

A gerund phrase includes the gerund, its modifiers, and the words that complete the idea begun by the gerund. In the following sentence, the simple gerund is in bold, the gerund phrase is underlined.

Swimming on our vacation was so much fun for the entire family.

Underline each gerund phrase once. Underline the gerund twice. Then identify whether the gerund in each sentence functions as a subject (S); predicate nominative (PN); direct object (DO), or object of a preposition (OP).

S 1. Studying art also taught Gerald about art history.
OP 2. Today was my first attempt at playing kickball.
S 3. Entering the contest was my mother's idea.
PN 4. Ava's next class is dancing.
S 5. Reporting the news is Jessica's dream job.
OP 6. Mrs. Palmer was given an award for volunteering her time.
S 7. Being the secretary of the art club is such a big responsibility.
S 8. Pressing the wrong button on this computer can be quite dangerous.
DO 9. Alberto prefers taking photos of landscapes.

36

Decimals & Percents

Any decimal can be converted to a percent by simply moving the decimal two places to the right and adding a percent sign. When a decimal contains thousandths or smaller percents, still move the decimal two places to the right. The percent will contain a decimal point.

Examples:
Convert 23 to %
$\frac{23}{100}$ = 23%

Convert 943 to %
$\frac{943}{1000}$ = 94.3%

To convert percents to decimals, move the decimal point two places to the left, and remove the percentage sign.

Examples:
Convert 45%
.45

Convert 102%
1.02

Convert the decimals to percents, and the percents to decimals.

1. .6	**60%**	11. 119%	**.19**	21. .008	**.8%**	
2. .43	**43%**	12. 105%	**1.05**	22. 2.321	**232.1%**	
3. 91.6%	**.916**	13. .5	**50%**	23. 98.2%	**.982**	
4. .05	**5%**	14. 1.05	**105%**	24. .15	**15%**	
5. 3.11	**311%**	15. 101.75	**10,175%**	25. 33.5%	**.335**	
6. 6%	**.06**	16. .695	**69.5%**	26. 223.23	**22,323%**	
7. 8.955	**895.5%**	17. 1.943	**194.3%**	27. 3.4	**340%**	
8. .731	**73.1%**	18. 2%	**.02**	28. .997	**99.7%**	
9. .82	**82%**	19. .013	**1.3%**	29. .14	**14%**	
10. 56.85%	**.5685**	20. 41.46	**4146%**	30. 9.775	**977.5%**	

37

Figurative Language

Review the following definitions of various kinds of figurative language.

Similes Comparisons using connecting words, such as like, as, or seems.
Example: A smile like a sunbeam brightened her face.

Metaphors are comparisons that use no connecting words.
Example: The clouds are fluffy pillows.

Personification appears frequently in poetry as well as prose. Personification is giving human characteristics to things that are not human.
Example: The storm knocked on our windows.

Hyperbole is an obvious exaggeration used to emphasize a point or add excitement and/or humor to a story.
Example: The walk from the car to the doctor's office took forever with my broken toe.

Read each of the following statements. Identify which of the four figurative language terms it represents. Write the answer in the blank provided.

personification 1. The leaves danced across the yard.
personification 2. The old, silent house remembered the happy days when laughing children filled its rooms.
hyperbole 3. I am so hungry I could eat a horse.
metaphor 4. The pet dog is another child in the family.
simile 5. Jordan can be as quiet as a mouse sometimes.
metaphor 6. Madison's bedroom was a pig's sty before she cleaned it.
simile 7. Vincent is as sharp as a tack.
personification 8. Yvonne bent close to Margi's ear and whispered, "Be careful, the walls have ears."
hyperbole 9. If I've told you once, I've told you a million times to close the door.
metaphor 10. The students felt that the essay assignment was a piece of cake.

38

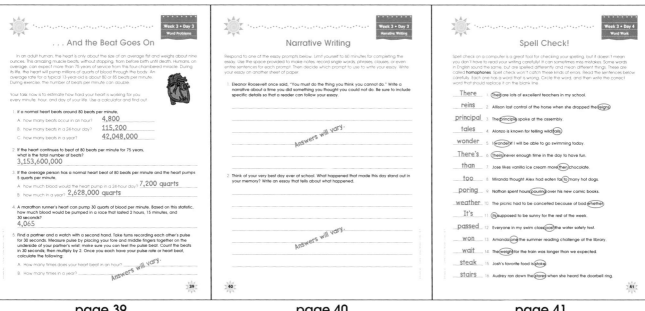

page 39   page 40   page 41

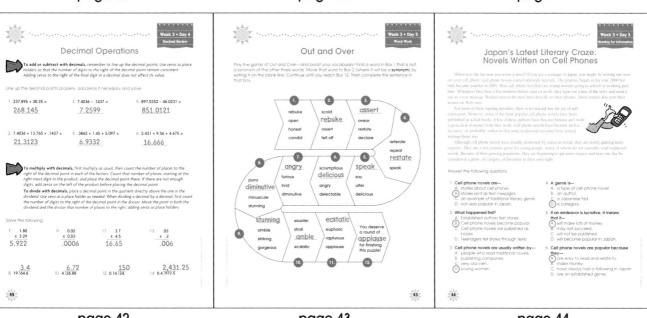

page 42   page 43   page 44

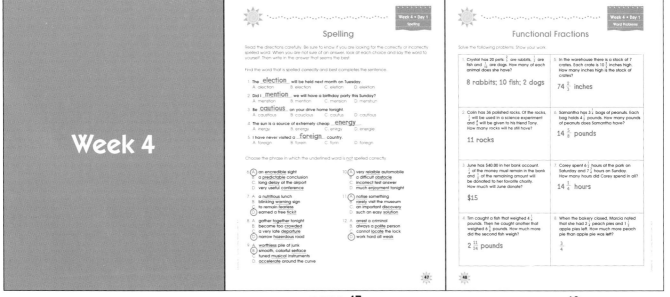

Week 4   page 47   page 48

page 49

Greek Roots

Many English words have Greek roots. Some examples are given in the chart below.

Greek Root	Meaning	Example
aero	air	aerate: expose to air or allow circulating air to reach or penetrate aerobics: system of exercises designed to increase respiration and heart rate
belli	war	rebellion: uprising belligerent: aggressive or warlike
pan	all	panorama: unlimited view panacea: a cure for all problems
chronos	time	chronic: lasting a long time synchronize: to happen at the same time

Use the chart to play Tic-Tac-Toe. Read each word. Then draw a line through three words in the box that are synonyms for that word. Your line can be vertical, horizontal, or diagonal.

panacea

cure-all	answer	solution
happiness	anger	ocean
physics	mix	air

synchronize

outdated	harmonious	disorderly
heavy	coincide	nonstop
wildly	coordinate	ancient

belligerent

pugnacious	loud	melodious
autonomy	aggressive	kind
coincide	chaos	combative

aerate

listen	angry	expose
yell	ventilate	forces
freshen	mix	rebellion

---

page 50

Geometry Jumble

Where is the world's oldest castle found?
To find out, unscramble each geometry word. Write the correctly spelled word in the spaces provided. The boxed letters from top to bottom reveal the location.

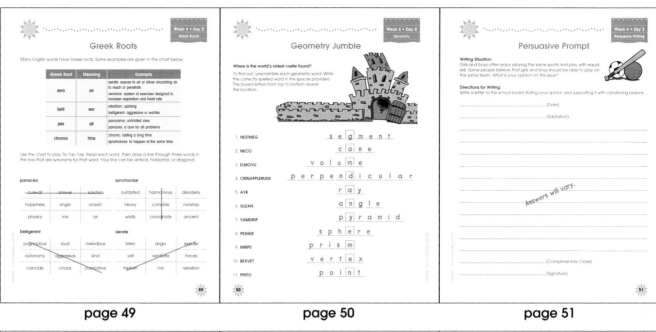

1. NESTMEG — s e g m e n t
2. NECO — c o n e
3. ELMOVU — v o l u m e
4. CRINAPPLERUDE — p e r p e n d i c u l a r
5. AYR — r a y
6. GLEAN — a n g l e
7. YAMDRIP — p y r a m i d
8. PESHER — s p h e r e
9. MIRPS — p r i s m
10. REXVET — v e r t e x
11. PINTO — p o i n t

---

page 51

Persuasive Prompt

Writing Situation:
Girls and boys often enjoy playing the same sports and play with equal skill. Some people believe that girls and boys should be able to play on the same team. What is your opinion on this issue?

Directions for Writing:
Write a letter to the school board stating your opinion and supporting it with convincing reasons.

_____ (Date)

_____ (Salutation)

_____

_____

_____

_____

Answers will vary.

_____

_____

_____ (Complimentary Close)

_____ (Signature)

---

page 52

Clothes Combos

How many combinations can you make with your favorite clothes? A tree diagram can show you. For example, Doug has one baseball cap, three shirts, and two pairs of pants. If he chooses one hat, one shirt, and one pair of pants for each outfit, how many outfits can he make?

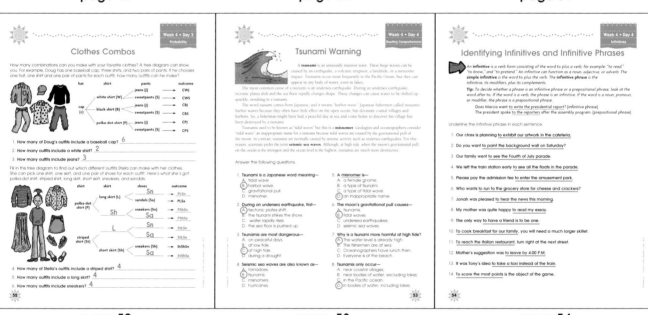

hat	shirt	pants	outcome
cap (c)	white shirt (W)	jeans (J)	CWJ
		sweatpants (S)	CWS
	black shirt (B)	jeans (J)	CBJ
		sweatpants (S)	CBS
	polka-dot shirt (P)	jeans (J)	CPJ
		sweatpants (S)	CPS

1. How many of Doug's outfits include a baseball cap? __6__
2. How many outfits include a white shirt? __2__
3. How many outfits include jeans? __3__

Fill in this tree diagram to find out which different outfits Stella can make with her clothes. She can pick one shirt, one skirt, and one pair of shoes for each outfit. Here's what she's got: polka-dot shirt, striped shirt, long skirt, short skirt, sneakers, and sandals.

shirt	skirt	shoes	outcome
polka-dot shirt (P)	long skirt (L)	Sn	PLSn
		sandals (Sa)	PLSa
	Sh	sneakers (Sn)	PShSn
		Sa	PShSa
striped shirt (St)	L	Sn	StLSn
		Sa	StLSa
	short skirt (Sh)	sneakers (Sh)	StShSn
		Sa	StShSa

4. How many of Stella's outfits include a striped shirt? __4__
5. How many outfits include a long skirt? __4__
6. How many outfits include sneakers? __4__

---

page 53

Tsunami Warning

A **tsunami** is an unusually massive wave. These huge waves can be caused by an earthquake, a volcanic eruption, a landslide, or a meteorite impact. Tsunamis occur most frequently in the Pacific Ocean, but they can appear in any body of water, even in lakes.

The most common cause of a tsunami is an undersea earthquake. During an undersea earthquake, tectonic plates shift and the sea floor rapidly changes shape. These changes can cause water to be shifted up quickly, resulting in a tsunami.

The word *tsunami* comes from Japanese, and it means "harbor wave." Japanese fishermen called tsunamis harbor waves because they often have little effect on the open ocean, but devastate coastal villages and harbors. So, a fisherman might have had a peaceful day at sea and come home to discover his village has been destroyed by a tsunami.

Tsunamis used to be known as "tidal waves" but this is a **misnomer**. Geologists and oceanographers consider "tidal wave" an inappropriate name for a tsunami because tidal waves are caused by the gravitational pull of the moon. In contrast, tsunamis are normally caused by seismic activity such as undersea earthquakes. For this reason, scientists prefer the term **seismic sea waves**. Although, at high tide, when the moon's gravitational pull on the ocean is the strongest and the ocean level is the highest, tsunamis are much more destructive.

Answer the following questions.

1. Tsunami is a Japanese word meaning—
   A. tidal wave.
   B. harbor wave.
   C. gravitational pull.
   D. misnomer.

2. During an undersea earthquake, first—
   A. tectonic plates shift.
   B. the tsunami strikes the shore.
   C. water rapidly rises.
   D. the sea floor is pushed up.

3. Tsunamis are most dangerous—
   A. on peaceful days.
   B. at low tide.
   C. at high tide.
   D. during a drought.

4. Seismic sea waves are also known as—
   A. tornadoes.
   B. tsunamis.
   C. misnomers.
   D. hurricanes.

5. A misnomer is—
   A. a female gnome.
   B. a type of tsunami.
   C. a type of tidal wave.
   D. an inappropriate name.

6. The moon's gravitational pull causes—
   A. tsunamis.
   B. tidal waves.
   C. undersea earthquakes.
   D. seismic sea waves.

7. Why is a tsunami more harmful at high tide?
   A. The water level is already high.
   B. The fishermen are at sea.
   C. Oceanographers have lunch then.
   D. Everyone is at the beach.

8. Tsunamis only occur—
   A. near coastal villages.
   B. near bodies of water, excluding lakes.
   C. in the Pacific ocean.
   D. in bodies of water, including lakes.

---

page 54

Identifying Infinitives and Infinitive Phrases

An **infinitive** is a verb form consisting of the word *to* plus a verb, for example: "to read," "to know," and "to pretend." An infinitive can function as a noun, adjective, or adverb. The **simple infinitive** is the word *to* plus the verb. The **infinitive phrase** is the infinitive, its modifiers, plus its complements.

Tip: To decide whether a phrase is an infinitive phrase or a prepositional phrase, look at the word after *to*. If the word is a verb, the phrase is an infinitive. If the word is a noun, pronoun, or modifier, the phrase is a prepositional phrase.

Does Marcia want to write the presidential report? (infinitive phrase)
The president spoke to the reporters after the assembly program. (prepositional phrase)

Underline the infinitive phrase in each sentence.

1. Our class is planning to exhibit our artwork in the cafeteria.
2. Do you want to paint the background wall on Saturday?
3. Our family went to see the Fourth of July parade.
4. We left the train station early to see all the floats in the parade.
5. Please pay the admission fee to enter the amusement park.
6. Who wants to run to the grocery store for cheese and crackers?
7. Jonah was pleased to hear the news this morning.
8. My mother was quite happy to read my essay.
9. The only way to have a friend is to be one.
10. To cook breakfast for our family, you will need a much larger skillet.
11. To reach the Italian restaurant, turn right at the next street.
12. Mother's suggestion was to leave by 4:00 P.M.
13. It was Tony's idea to take a taxi instead of the train.
14. To score the most points is the object of the game.

---

page 55

Car for Rent

Here's your chance to see the U.S.A.— without leaving your home!

The following car rental plans are from Take Off Rent-a-Car.

Plan A	Plan B	Plan C
$32.95 per day	$27.95 per day	$45 per day
500 free miles	no free miles	1,500 free miles
then $0.20 a mile	then $0.25 a mile	then $0.30 a mile

1. Choose a North American destination you'd like to visit. How about the Statue of Liberty, Big Bend National Park, Monument Valley, or the Everglades? Plot a route to the spot you pick. Map out and record the route and estimate the driving distance.

2. Figure out how long the entire round-trip would take. Remember: You can't drive all day long, and you need to sleep, eat, get gas, and spend some time at the place you're visiting. And don't forget those speed limits!

Answers will vary.

3. Using each plan, determine the cost of the car rental for your entire round-trip. Which plan makes the most sense for you? Why?

---

page 56

Pedal Power

On Monday mornings, city streets are jammed with cars and buses filled with commuters. Take a closer look, and you might see plenty of people pedaling their way to work or school. The number of bike commuters has more than tripled over the past two decades. Worldwide, three times more bikes are built than cars.

Why do so many Americans like to ride bikes? Biking is a fun way to get outdoors and to exercise. More people are discovering that on a bike, they can get in shape and get where they need to go at the same time. In fact, nearly five million Americans commute to work on bicycles.

Two major bike-to-work cities are Tucson, Arizona, and San Diego, California. In these areas, warm weather makes year-round biking possible. Surprisingly, rainy Seattle, Washington, and chilly Minneapolis, Minnesota, both have high rates of bicycle commuters.

Cities are racing to make the ride easier. More bike commuters mean fewer cars. Fewer cars can mean less of a need for new roads. Creating bike paths or "Bikes Only" lanes on streets is far less expensive than building roads.

Officials in Portland, Oregon, came up with a unique idea. They wanted to encourage people to bike around town instead of driving. So the city rounded up used bikes—ones that people would have just thrown away. They repaired them and painted them yellow. Then they put the yellow bikes around the city and spread the word that they were free for anyone to use. When borrowers reach their destination, they just leave the bike for someone else. People are pedaling the yellow bikes all over Portland. The public bike fleet is growing as more people donate old bikes. Will your town be next? About 50 cities have asked Portland how to start their own public pedal-power program!

All of these healthy bikers help create a healthier environment. When it comes to planet-friendly modes of transportation, you can't beat a bike. Unlike cars, bikes burn no fossil fuels and create no air pollution. In addition, computer-aided design and new technologies have helped create a new breed of bicycles that make riding safer, easier, and a lot more fun.

Write one paragraph summarizing what you read in "Pedal Power."

Answers will vary.

Week 5

Week 5 • Day 1
Variables

Evaluating Variable Expressions

*In math, a **variable** is a letter used to represent one or more numbers in a mathematical expression.*

Example: Evaluate $\frac{22}{y}$ when y = 2
$\frac{22}{2} = 11$

Evaluate each expression when y = 2.

1. 8y 16
2. $\frac{10}{y}$ 5
3. y + 3 5
4. 14 – y 12

Evaluate each expression when y = 5.

5. 2y – 3 7
6. y + y + 8 18
7. 19 – y + 4 18
8. 9 – y + 3 – 1 6

The perimeter of a square is equal to 4s where s equals the length of one side.

9. What is the perimeter of a square where s is equal to 7 feet? 28
10. Find the perimeter of a square where s = 123 feet. 492
11. James knows the perimeter of a square is 1,023 feet. He stated that one side of the square is an even whole number. Is this answer correct? Why or why not?
No. Because for the sides to be an even number, the perimeter would have to be an even number divisible by 4. 1023 is an odd number and cannot be divided evenly by 4.

59

page 59

Week 5 • Day 1
Following Directions

Comparing Family Recipes

These one-dish meals are easy to prepare. Add a salad, bread, beverage, and dessert, and dinner is served! With permission, you can be chef for a day and prepare dinner for the family at least twice this summer. After each meal, have each family member evaluate the hot dish. Allow the members of your family to vote to decide if the dish should be added to the family's favorites. Things to consider are as follows: taste, cost per serving, ease of preparation, and possible leftovers.

Read the recipe below. Then answer the questions.

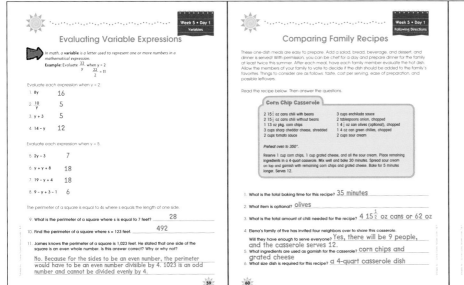

Corn Chip Casserole

2 $15\frac{1}{2}$ oz cans chili with beans
2 $15\frac{1}{2}$ oz cans chili without beans
1 13 oz pkg. corn chips
3 cups sharp cheddar cheese, shredded
2 cups tomato sauce
3 cups enchilada sauce
2 tablespoons onion, chopped
1 $4\frac{1}{2}$ oz can olives (optional), chopped
1 4 oz can green chilies, chopped
2 cups sour cream

Preheat oven to 350°.

Reserve 1 cup corn chips, 1 cup grated cheese, and all the sour cream. Place remaining ingredients in a 4-quart casserole. Mix well and bake 30 minutes. Spread sour cream on top and garnish with remaining corn chips and grated cheese. Bake for 5 minutes longer. Serves 12.

1. What is the total baking time for this recipe? 35 minutes
2. What item is optional? olives
3. What is the total amount of chili needed for the recipe? 4 $15\frac{1}{2}$ oz cans or 62 oz
4. Elena's family of five has invited four neighbors over to share this casserole. Will they have enough to serve everyone? Yes, there will be 9 people, and the casserole serves 12.
5. What ingredients are used as garnish for the casserole? corn chips and grated cheese
6. What size dish is required for this recipe? a 4-quart casserole dish

60

page 60

Week 5 • Day 2
Descriptive Writing

Show, Don't Tell

When you show, rather than tell, in your writing, you help readers create pictures in their minds. Review the examples to see the difference.

Examples:

Telling	Showing
Jill was happy.	Jill skipped down the hall, clapping her hands and smiling at everyone.
The puppy was scared.	Shivering and whimpering, the puppy cowered behind the couch during the storm.

Rewrite the following sentences so that you are showing, rather than telling.

1. My room was a mess.
2. Summer camp was fun.
3. Making cupcakes left a big mess in the kitchen.
Answers will vary.
4. The soccer game was bad.
5. The dinner was good.

61

page 61

Week 5 • Day 2
Estimation

Estimation: Using Rounding

Solve the problems below, using only estimation. Using a calculator, pencil, or paper is not allowed. Round your answers to the nearest dollar.

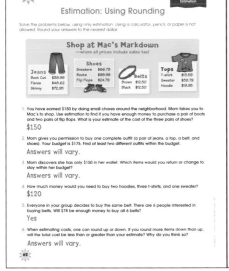

Shop at Mac's Markdown
—where all prices include sales tax!
Jeans
Boot Cut $39.99
Flares $48.62
Skinny $72.95
Shoes
Sneakers $66.78
Boots $99.99
Flip Flops $24.79
Belts
Brown $12.50
Black $12.50
Tops
T-shirt $13.59
Sweater $38.79
Hoodie $19.95

1. You have earned $150 by doing small chores around the neighborhood. Mom takes you to Mac's to shop. Use estimation to find if you have enough money to purchase a pair of boots and two pairs of flip flops. What is your estimate of the cost of the three pairs of shoes?
$150
2. Mom gives you permission to buy one complete outfit (a pair of jeans, a top, a belt, and shoes). Your budget is $175. Find at least two different outfits within the budget.
Answers will vary.
3. Mom discovers she has only $150 in her wallet. Which items would you return or change to stay within her budget?
Answers will vary.
4. How much money would you need to buy two hoodies, three t-shirts, and one sweater?
$120
5. Everyone in your group decides to buy the same belt. There are 6 people interested in buying belts. Will $78 be enough money to buy all 6 belts?
Yes
6. When estimating costs, one can round up or down. If you round more items down than up, will the total cost be less than or greater than your estimate? Why do you think so?
Answers will vary.

62

page 62

Week 5 • Day 3
Portmanteau

Blends

*When parts of two words are combined, the new word that is formed is called a **blend**, or a **portmanteau**. Examples of some blends are given in the chart below.*

Word One	Word Two	Blend
smoke	fog	smog
emotion	icon	emoticon
breakfast	lunch	brunch
chuckle	snort	chortle
flout	vaunt	flaunt

Write the blend formed from each pair of words below.

1. motor and hotel motel
2. situation and comedy sitcom
3. information and commercial infomercial
4. walk and marathon walkathon
5. splash and spatter splatter

Write the best blend from the chart above to complete each sentence.

6. Aiden ended his text message with a funny emoticon.
7. On weekends, brunch is served in the restaurant after 11am.
8. Alissa likes to flaunt her diving skills.
9. The fire added to the layer of smog over the city.
10. The audience began to chortle when the comedian told the joke.

63

page 63

Week 5 • Day 3
Parts of Speech

Identifying Parts of Speech

Identify the parts of speech in italics by labeling it **n.** (noun), **pro.** (pronoun), **v.** (verb), **adj.** (adjective), **adv.** (adverb), **prep.** (preposition), **conj.** (conjunction), and **interj.** (interjection).

interj. 1. *Oh,* I left my purse and cell phone on the seat in my aunt's car.
prep. 2. *During* the party, our dog had to stay outside the house.
v. 3. Old Faithful geyser *erupts* almost hourly.
adv. 4. The race car drove *extremely* fast.
conj. 5. *Neither* Sonja *nor* Isabelle wants to go swimming.
prep. 6. Joe and Maria usually play softball *with* Terry and Thomas.
pro. 7. *Who* told you about our trip to Spain?
conj. 8. Molly vacuumed the carpets, *and* I cleaned the windows.
interj. 9. *Ouch!* I did not know the edge of the board was so sharp.
v. 10. Yesterday we *walked* through the park on the way home.
prep. 11. You must make a decision *before* six o'clock.
pro. 12. *They* mow lawns during the summer to earn extra money.
adv. 13. Which of the two movies did you like *better*?
adj. 14. The *oldest* clock in the world is in England.
v. 15. My little brother *went* to play softball in the park.
pro. 16. The red brick house on the corner is *ours*.

64

page 64

Week 5 • Day 4
Basic Operations

Practice Makes Perfect

Solve the problems. Pay attention to the signs. You can use a calculator.

1. 126 x 6 = 756
2. 2,972 – 984 = 1,988
3. 92,475 – 76,097 = 16,378
4. 22,048 + 31,456 = 53,504
5. 242 x 33 = 7,986
6. 7785 ÷ 45 = 173
7. 39,995 + 12,699 = 52,694
8. 926 x 27 = 25,002
9. 5280 ÷ 120 = 44
10. 19,191 + 91,999 = 111,190
11. 11,925 ÷ 225 = 53
12. 507 x 109 = 55,263
13. 52,009 – 21,950 = 30,059
14. 108,462 ÷ 2 = 54,231
15. 2011 x 66 = 132,726

To find the answer to this riddle, solve the math problem using your calculator. Then turn the calculator so you can read the answer upside down.

What flies but is not a plane, floats but is not a ship, and honks but is not a truck?

Solve:
50 x 7 x 100 + 9 = 35,009 GOOSE

65

page 65

Week 5 • Day 4
Algebra

Evaluating Algebraic Expressions

When evaluating an algebraic expression:
First, substitute the numbers for the variables.
Then solve the resulting equation.

Example: m = 4 t = 3
7m – 3t =
(7 • 4) – (3 • 3)
28 – 9
19

Evaluate the algebraic expressions below using the following values: p = 15, t = 3, r = 2, m = 4.

1. 10 m – (p + 9) – r = 14
2. p (11m + 7t) – 975 = 0
3. 2p + 6t + 7r = 62
4. $\frac{4p}{m-1}$ 20
5. $\frac{6t}{r}$ 9
6. 2tm 24
7. (pt) (rm) 360
8. pr ÷ 3 10

66

page 66

Use with page 68.
Week 5 • Day 5
Reading Comprehension

The Disappearing Bees

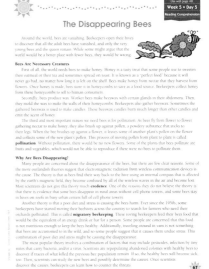

Around the world, bees are vanishing. Beekeepers open their hives to discover that all the adult bees have vanished, and only the very young bees and the queen remain. While some might argue that the world would be a better place with fewer bees, they would be wrong.

Bees Are Necessary Creatures

First of all, the world needs bees to make honey. Honey is a tasty treat that some people use to sweeten their oatmeal or their tea and sometimes spread on toast. It is known as a "perfect food" because it will never go bad, no matter how long it is left on the shelf. Bees make honey from nectar that they harvest from flowers. Once honey is made, bees store it in honeycombs to save as a food source. Beekeepers collect honey from these honeycombs to sell to human consumers.

Secondly, bees produce wax. Worker bees make beeswax with certain glands in their abdomens. Then, they mold the wax to make the walls of their honeycombs. Beekeepers also gather beeswax. Sometimes the gathered beeswax is used to make candles. These beeswax candles burn much longer than other candles and emit the scent of honey.

The third and most important reason we need bees is for pollination. As bees fly from flower to flower gathering nectar to make honey, they also brush up against pollen, a powdery substance that sticks to their legs. When the bee brushes up against a flower, it leaves some of another plant's pollen on the flower and collects some of the new plant's pollen. This process of moving pollen from plant to plant is called **pollination**. Without pollination, there would be no new flowers. Some of the plants that bees pollinate are fruits and vegetables, which would not be able to reproduce if there were no bees to pollinate them.

Why Are Bees Disappearing?

Many people are concerned about the disappearance of the bees, but there are few clear reasons. Some of the more outlandish theories suggest that electromagnetic radiation from wireless communication devices is the cause. The theory is that as bees find their way back to the hive using an internal compass that is affected by the earth's magnetic field, they become confused by all of the wireless waves in the air and become lost. Most scientists do not give this theory much **credence**. One of the reasons they do not believe the theory is that there is evidence that some bees disappear in rural areas without cell phone towers, and some bees stay in hives on roofs in busy urban centers full of cell phone towers.

Another theory is that a poor diet and stress is causing the bees harm. Ever since the 1950s, some beekeepers have started moving their beehives across the country to search for farmers who need their orchards pollinated. This is called **migratory beekeeping**. These roving beekeepers feed their bees food that would be the equivalent of an energy drink or bar for a person. Some people are concerned that this food is not nutritious enough to keep the bees healthy. Additionally, traveling around in vans is not something that bees are accustomed to in the wild, and so some people suggest that it causes them undue stress. This combination of poor diet and stress might be causing the disappearance.

The most popular theory involves a combination of factors that may include pesticides, infection by tiny mites that carry bacteria, and/or a virus. Scientists are repopulating abandoned colonies with healthy bees to discover if traces of what killed the previous bee population remain. If so, the healthy bees will become sick, too. Then, scientists can study the new bees and possibly determine the causes. Once scientists discover the causes, beekeepers can learn how to counter the threats.

67

page 67

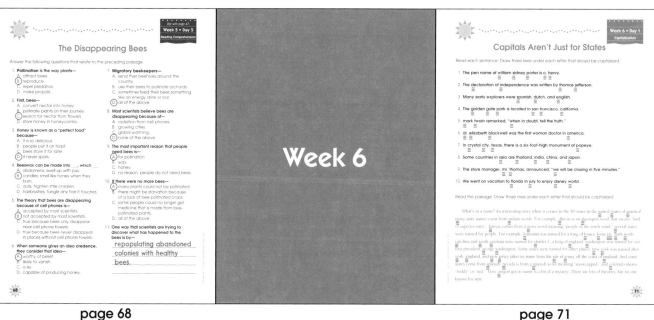

Use with page 67.
Week 5 • Day 5
Reading Comprehension

The Disappearing Bees

Answer the following questions that relate to the preceding passage.

1. **Pollination is the way plants—**
   A. attract bees.
   (B.) reproduce.
   C. repel predators.
   D. make propolis.
2. **First, bees—**
   A. convert nectar into honey.
   B. pollinate plants on their journey.
   (C.) search for nectar from flowers.
   D. store honey in honeycombs.
3. **Honey is known as a "perfect food" because—**
   A. it is so delicious.
   B. people put it on toast.
   C. bees store it for later.
   (D.) it never spoils.
4. **Beeswax can be made into ___, which ___**
   A. abdomens; swell up with pus.
   (B.) candles; smell like honey when they burn.
   C. dolls; frighten little children.
   D. hairbrushes; tangle any hair it touches.
5. **The theory that bees are disappearing because of cell phones is—**
   A. accepted by most scientists.
   (B.) not accepted by most scientists.
   C. true because bees only disappear near cell phone towers.
   D. true because bees never disappear in places without cell phone towers.
6. **When someone gives an idea credence, they consider that idea—**
   (A.) worthy of belief.
   B. likely to vanish.
   C. a lie.
   D. capable of producing honey.
7. **Migratory beekeepers—**
   A. send their beehives around the country.
   B. use their bees to pollinate orchards.
   C. sometimes feed their bees something like an energy drink or bar.
   (D.) all of the above
8. **Most scientists believe bees are disappearing because of—**
   A. radiation from cell phones.
   B. growing cities.
   C. global warming.
   (D.) none of the above
9. **The most important reason that people need bees is—**
   (A.) for pollination.
   B. wax.
   C. honey.
   D. no reason, people do not need bees.
10. **If there were no more bees—**
    (A.) many plants could not be pollinated.
    B. there might be starvation because of a lack of bee-pollinated crops.
    C. some people could no longer get medicine that is made from bee-pollinated plants.
    D. all of the above
11. **One way that scientists are trying to discover what has happened to the bees is by—**
    repopulating abandoned colonies with healthy bees.

page 68

Week 6

Week 6 • Day 1
Capitalization

Capitals Aren't Just for States

Read each sentence. Draw three lines under each letter that should be capitalized.

1. The pen name of william sidney porter is o. henry.
2. The declaration of independence was written by thomas jefferson.
3. Many early explorers were spanish, dutch, and english.
4. The golden gate park is located in san francisco, california.
5. mark twain remarked, "when in doubt, tell the truth."
6. dr. elizabeth blackwell was the first woman doctor in america.
7. In crystal city, texas, there is a six-foot-high monument of popeye.
8. Some countries in asia are thailand, india, china, and japan.
9. The store manager, mr. thomas, announced, "we will be closing in five minutes."
10. We went on vacation to florida in july to enjoy disney world.

Read the passage. Draw three lines under each letter that should be capitalized.

What's in a name? An interesting story when it comes to the 50 states in the united states of america! many state names come from indian words. For example, illinois is an algonquin word that means "land of superior men." kansas comes from a sioux word meaning "people of the south wind." several states were named for people. For example, louisiana was named for a king of france, louis xiv. both north carolina and south carolina were named for charles I, a king of england. washington was named for our first president, george washington. Some states were named for other places. new york was named after york, england, and new jersey takes its name from the isle of jersey off the coast of england. And some states come from spanish. nevada is from a spanish word meaning "snowcapped," and colorado means "ruddy" or "red." How oregon got its name is a bit of a mystery. There are lots of theories, but no one knows for sure.

page 71

Week 6 • Day 1
Reading a Chart

Counting Calories

A calorie is a unit of energy that humans receive from the food they eat. Do you know how many calories are in some of your favorite foods? The calorie chart below gives average calorie counts for some common foods.

Calorie Chart

	Calories		Calories
1 medium apple	70	1 cup ice cream	270
1 medium banana	100	1 cup skim milk	120
2 slices white bread	140	1 cup whole milk	150
1 regular cheeseburger	518	1 medium orange	65
$\frac{1}{4}$ cup dry, unsweetened cereal	70	1 cup orange juice	120
4 ounces baked chicken	205	1 slice cheese pizza	145
1 cup cola (soda)	145	3 pancakes	180
4 plain sugar cookies	200	1 cup unbuttered popcorn	25
10 French fries	135	15 potato chips	150
1 fried egg	115	1 cup spaghetti and sauce	260
1 hot dog	291	$\frac{3}{4}$ cup tuna fish salad	210

Find Justin's calorie intake for two days. Add each day's calories and then answer the questions.

Day 1		Calories
Breakfast:	3 pancakes	180
	1 cup orange juice	120
Lunch:	20 French fries	270
	1 cheeseburger	518
	1 cup whole milk	150
	4 cookies	200
Dinner:	3 slices of pizza	435
	2 cups soda	290
	1 cup ice cream	270
Snack:	30 potato chips	300
	TOTAL CALORIES	2,733

Day 2		Calories
Breakfast:	$\frac{1}{4}$ cup dry cereal	70
	1 cup skim milk	120
	1 cup orange juice	120
Lunch:	$\frac{3}{4}$ cup tuna salad	210
	2 slices white bread	140
	1 cup skim milk	120
Dinner:	1 medium apple	70
	1 cup spaghetti	260
	1 cup skim milk	120
	1 medium orange	65
Snack:	1 cup popcorn	25
	TOTAL CALORIES	1,320

On which day did Justin consume fewer calories? Day 2

What was the difference in calorie intake between days 1 and 2? 1,413 calories

page 72

Week 6 • Day 2
Types of Sentences

Identifying Types of Sentences

A **simple sentence** *has one independent clause and no dependent clauses. It has a subject and a predicate, but these may be compound.*

Example: The roller coaster and the terror tower are the most popular rides in the park.

A **compound sentence** *has two or more independent clauses joined together, but no dependent clauses. The clauses may be joined by a comma and a coordinating conjunction or by a semicolon. Examples of coordinating conjunctions are* **and**, **but**, **or**, **nor**, *or* **for**.

Example: Frankie wanted to ride the Ferris wheel, **but** Anna was afraid.

A **complex sentence** *has one independent clause and one or more dependent clauses. Many dependent clauses are introduced by subordinating conjunctions. Examples of subordinating conjunctions are* **after**, **although**, **as**, **as soon as**, **because**, **before**, **even though**, **if**, **since**, **when**, *and* **until**.

After studying the definitions and examples of the types of sentences, identify each sentence below with **S** for simple, **CD** for compound, and **CX** for complex.

S 1. Deja opened her book and raised her hand.
CD 2. The rain stopped suddenly, and the cold air rushed in from the mountains.
S 3. A severe thunderstorm struck the downtown area and interrupted power for hours.
CX 4. As darkness closed in around the campfire, the campers began to shiver.
CX 5. When I saw the word in the book, I had to look it up in the dictionary.
S 6. Jessica asked the store manager for directions to the new mall.
CD 7. Mario took the flag down, and Angela folded it.
CX 8. No one ever entered the old house because people thought it was haunted.
CX 9. After the baseball game ends, we will eat dinner at a nearby restaurant.
CD 10. Aldo heard strange noises, but they did not frighten him.

page 73

Week 6 • Day 2
Expository Writing

"How To" Prompt

Often the most difficult thing about teaching someone "how-to" do something is being precise and concise with the explanation and step-by-step instructions. Think about your favorite pastime. It may be playing a sport, participating in a hobby, or creating something.

Write a composition that explains to someone else the background of your interest in the activity and how to accomplish it. Be sure that you include all of the details needed to do the activity. When you feel the directions are complete, reread them and make corrections and adjustments. Finally, have someone else read and, if possible, follow your directions. How successful a teacher were you?

How to ______________________

Answers will vary.

page 74

Week 6 • Day 3
Using Formulas

Bone Up on Formulas

To a forensic scientist, a skeleton isn't just a pile of old bones. It's a clue! Sometimes, a scientist may have only one bone to study. But thanks to formulas, even that can be enough to find out information such as how tall the person was when he or she was alive.

Take a look at the real-life forensic formulas below. Then use them to answer the questions.

Forensic Formulas for Height

In these formulas, r = radius, h = humerus, and t = tibia. All measurements are in centimeters (cm).

Male:
$80.4 + 3.7r = \text{height}$
$73.6 + 3.0h = \text{height}$
$81.7 + 2.4t = \text{height}$

Female:
$73.5 + 3.9r = \text{height}$
$65.0 + 3.1h = \text{height}$
$72.6 + 2.5t = \text{height}$

1. **A forensic scientist is given the tibia of a woman who lived hundreds of years ago, found at an archaeological dig. What formula should the scientist use to find out how tall the woman was?**
   $72.6 + 2.5t$
2. **If the tibia from question 1 was 37 cm long, how tall was the woman?**
   165.1 cm
3. **Suppose police find a man's tibia that is 46 cm long. How tall was he?**
   192.1 cm
4. **Say a woman's humerus, 28 cm long, is discovered. How tall was she?** 151.8 cm
5. **A forensic scientist finds a man's radius, 31 cm long. How tall was he?** 195.1 cm

page 75

Week 6 • Day 3
Tricky Words

Confusing Word Choices

Some words are often confused because they sound similar, even though they are not pronounced exactly the same way and have different spellings and meanings. Look closely at the context of each sentence to determine the correct word choice. If needed, use a dictionary.

Underline the word that best completes each sentence.

1. Once the program started, everyone became (quiet, quite).
2. Jennifer cannot decide (wither, whether) to practice her piano lessons or to play soccer.
3. My mother drove (pest, past) Mr. Choo on her way home from work.
4. Dessert is the sweet (course, cores) usually served at the end of a meal.
5. The valedictorian deserved all of the (prize, praise) and adoration she received.
6. Kelly ate the last (peas, piece) of chocolate cake.
7. Everyone on the swim team was able to practice (accept, except) Corey, who was sick.
8. Last summer, we chose to visit Boston, the (capital, capitol) of Massachusetts.
9. Don't forget to bring your camera to take (pitchers, pictures) on our vacation.
10. Of all the people who live on our street, Mrs. Martinez is the loudest (singer, zinger).
11. Isabella saw many (ilk, elk) in Yellowstone National Park this summer.
12. It was interesting to hear about my brother's (signs, science) experiment.

page 76

Week 6 • Day 4
Reading Comprehension

The *Mona Lisa's* Hardships

The *Mona Lisa* is one of the most famous paintings in the world. Leonardo da Vinci painted this portrait of a Renaissance woman in oil on a panel of poplar wood. Although most people are familiar with the lady's smile, they may be surprised at what this painting has survived in its 500 years.

The *Mona Lisa* has seen a great deal in its lifetime. Originally, the portrait hung in the chateau of the King of France, where noblemen and dignitaries could admire it. Later, it graced the wall of Napoleon Bonaparte's bedroom. After the French Revolution, the painting moved to the **Louvre**, an art museum in Paris, France. At the museum, millions of people could come to enjoy the *Mona Lisa's* artistry.

During the Second World War, the *Mona Lisa* was spirited away to safety. It finally landed in Montauben, a city in southern France. Unfortunately, while it was displayed there in 1956, someone splashed acid on it. Later that same year, a man threw a rock at the painting. Both of these acts of **vandalism** led to costly, careful repairs to the painting. The painting now rests at the Louvre behind bulletproof glass to prevent further damage.

By far the most dramatic attack on the *Mona Lisa* occurred when it was stolen in 1911. The police tracked down many leads and investigated everyone from visitors to cleaning staff and security guards. Still, for two long years, they found nothing but dead ends. In 1913, the thief, Vincenzo Peruggia, was caught trying to sell the treasured painting to an antique dealer in Florence, Italy. Finally, the lost lady was found! The painting toured several major cities before being returned to the Louvre, where it remains to this day.

Answer the following questions.

1. **The *Mona Lisa*—**
   A. rests in the Louvre, in Paris, France.
   B. is a painting by Leonardo da Vinci.
   C. is a national treasure for the French.
   (D.) all of the above
2. **Da Vinci's *Mona Lisa* is painted—**
   A. on canvas.
   (B.) on poplar wood.
   C. with pastels.
   D. with a moustache.
3. **When the *Mona Lisa* was hung in the King of France's chateau, it was viewed by—**
   A. millions of people everyday.
   B. Vincenzo Peruggia everyday.
   C. the King only.
   (D.) noblemen and dignitaries only.
4. **If you made a timeline of the *Mona Lisa's* hardships, which of the following happened first?**
   A. the *Mona Lisa* had a rock thrown at it.
   B. the *Mona Lisa* had acid splashed on it.
   C. the *Mona Lisa* survived World War II.
   (D.) the *Mona Lisa* was stolen by Peruggia.
5. **The Louvre is—**
   A. the bedroom of Napoleon Bonaparte.
   B. an art museum in Paris, France.
   C. the home of the Mona Lisa.
   (D.) both B and C.
6. **The definition of vandalism is probably—**
   A. careful repairs to paintings.
   B. stealing paintings.
   C. cleaning up property.
   (D.) willful destruction of property.

page 77

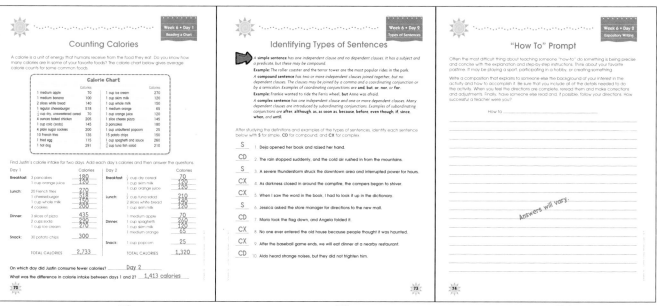

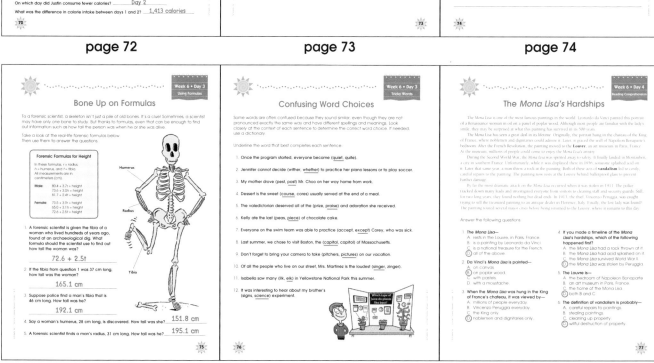

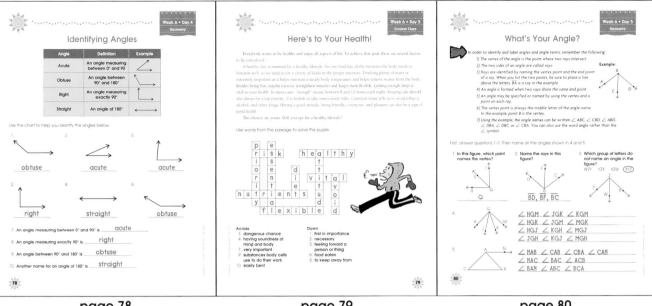

page 78

Identifying Angles

Angle	Definition	Example
Acute	An angle measuring between 0° and 90°	
Obtuse	An angle between 90° and 180°	
Right	An angle measuring exactly 90°	
Straight	An angle of 180°	

Use the chart to help you identify the angles below.

1. obtuse
3. acute
5. acute
2. right
4. straight
6. obtuse

7. An angle measuring between 0° and 90° is acute
8. An angle measuring exactly 90° is right
9. An angle between 90° and 180° is obtuse
10. Another name for an angle of 180° is straight

page 79

Here's to Your Health!

Everybody wants to be healthy and enjoy all aspects of life. To achieve that goal, there are several factors to be considered.

A healthy diet is essential for a healthy lifestyle. No one food has all the nutrients the body needs to function well, so we need to eat a variety of foods in the proper amounts. Drinking plenty of water is extremely important as it helps maintain a steady body temperature and helps remove wastes from the body. Besides being fun, regular exercise strengthens muscles and keeps them flexible. Getting enough sleep is vital to your health. In most cases, "enough" means between 8 and 12 hours each night. Keeping safe should also always be a top priority. It is foolish to take unnecessary risks. Common sense tells us to avoid tobacco, alcohol, and other drugs. Having a good attitude, being friendly, courteous, and pleasant can also be a sign of good health.

The choices are yours. Will you opt for a healthy lifestyle?

Use words from the passage to solve the puzzle.

Across
3. dangerous chance
4. having soundness of mind and body
7. very important
9. substances body cells use to do their work
10. easily bent

Down
1. first in importance
2. necessary
5. feeling toward a person or thing
6. food eaten
8. to keep away from

page 80

What's Your Angle?

In order to identify and label angles and angle terms, remember the following:
1) The vertex of the angle is the point where two rays intersect.
2) The two sides of an angle are called rays.
3) Rays are identified by naming the vertex point and the end point of a ray. When you list the two points, be sure to place a line above the letters. BA is a ray in the example.
4) An angle is formed when two rays share the same end point.
5) An angle may be specified or named by using the vertex and a point on each ray.
6) The vertex point is always the middle letter of the angle name. In the example, point B is the vertex.
7) Using the example, the angle names can be written ∠ ABC, ∠ CBD, ∠ ABD, ∠ DBA, ∠ DBC, or ∠ CBA. You can also use the word angle rather than the ∠ symbol.

First, answer questions 1-3. Then name all the angles shown in 4 and 5.

1. In this figure, which point names the vertex? Q
2. Name the rays in this figure? BD, BF, BC
3. Which group of letters do *not* name an angle in the figure? WZY YZX XZW (XYZ)

4. ∠ HGM ∠ JGK ∠ KGM
   ∠ HGK ∠ JGM ∠ MGK
   ∠ HGJ ∠ KGH ∠ MGJ
   ∠ JGH ∠ KGJ ∠ MGH

5. ∠ NAB ∠ CAB ∠ CBA ∠ CAN
   ∠ NAC ∠ BAC ∠ ACB
   ∠ BAN ∠ ABC ∠ BCA

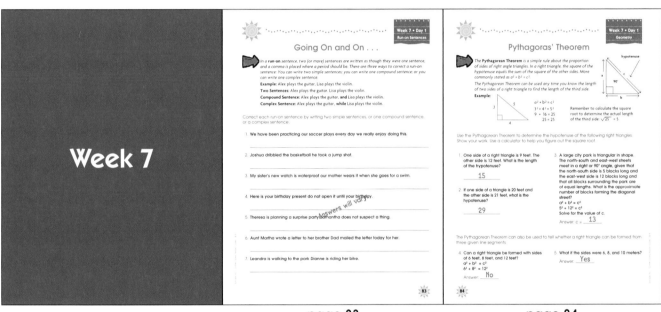

Week 7

page 83

Going On and On . . .

In a **run-on** sentence, two (or more) sentences are written as though they were one sentence, and a comma is placed where a period should be. There are three ways to correct a run-on sentence: You can write two simple sentences; you can write one compound sentence; or you can write one complex sentence.
Example: Alex plays the guitar. Lisa plays the violin.
Two Sentences: Alex plays the guitar. Lisa plays the violin.
Compound Sentence: Alex plays the guitar, **and** Lisa plays the violin.
Complex Sentence: Alex plays the guitar, **while** Lisa plays the violin.

Correct each run-on sentence by writing two simple sentences, or one compound sentence, or a complex sentence.

1. We have been practicing our soccer plays every day we really enjoy doing this.

2. Joshua dribbled the basketball he took a jump shot.

3. My sister's new watch is waterproof my mother wears it when she goes for a swim.

4. Here is your birthday present do not open it until your birthday.

5. Theresa is planning a surprise party Samantha does not suspect a thing.

6. Aunt Martha wrote a letter to her brother Dad mailed the letter today for her.

7. Leandra is walking to the park Dianne is riding her bike.

Answers will vary.

page 84

Pythagoras' Theorem

The **Pythagorean Theorem** is a simple rule about the proportion of sides of right angle triangles. In a right triangle, the square of the hypotenuse equals the sum of the square of the other sides. More commonly stated as $a^2 + b^2 = c^2$.
The Pythagorean Theorem can be used any time you know the length of two sides of a right triangle to find the length of the third side.

Example:
$$a^2 + b^2 = c^2$$
$$3^2 + 4^2 = 5^2$$
$$9 + 16 = 25$$
$$25 = 25$$

Remember to calculate the square root to determine the actual length of the third side. $\sqrt{25} = 5$

Use the Pythagorean Theorem to determine the hypotenuse of the following right triangles. Show your work. Use a calculator to help you figure out the square root.

1. One side of a right triangle is 9 feet. The other side is 12 feet. What is the length of the hypotenuse? 15

2. If one side of a triangle is 20 feet and the other side is 21 feet, what is the hypotenuse? 29

3. A large city park is triangular in shape. The north-south and east-west streets meet in a right or 90° angle, given that the north-south side is 5 blocks long and the east-west side is 12 blocks long and that all blocks surrounding the park are of equal lengths. What is the approximate number of blocks forming the diagonal street?
$$a^2 + b^2 = c^2$$
$$5^2 + 12^2 = c^2$$
Solve for the value of c.
Answer: c = 13

The Pythagorean Theorem can also be used to tell whether a right triangle can be formed from three given line segments.

4. Can a right triangle be formed with sides of 6 feet, 8 feet, and 12 feet?
$$a^2 + b^2 = c^2$$
$$6^2 + 8^2 = 12^2$$
Answer: No

5. What if the sides were 6, 8, and 10 meters?
Answer: Yes

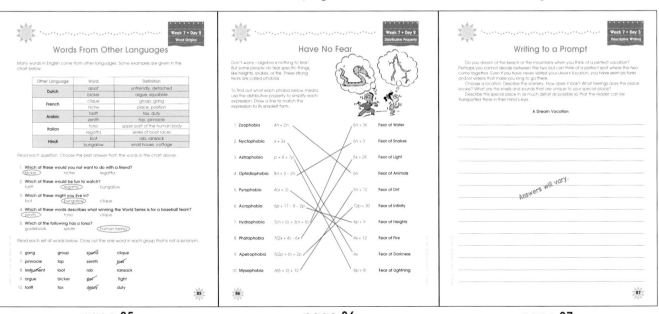

page 85

Words From Other Languages

Many words in English come from other languages. Some examples are given in the chart below.

Other Language	Word	Definition
Dutch	aloof	unfriendly, detached
	bicker	argue, squabble
French	clique	group, gang
	niche	place, position
Arabic	tariff	tax, duty
	zenith	top, pinnacle
Italian	torso	upper part of the human body
	regatta	series of boat races
Hindi	loot	rob, ransack
	bungalow	small house, cottage

Read each question. Choose the best answer from the words in the chart above.

1. Which of these would you not want to do with a friend? (bicker) niche regatta
2. Which of these would be fun to watch? tariff (regatta) bungalow
3. Which of these might you live in? loot (bungalow) clique
4. Which of these words describes what winning the World Series is for a baseball team? (zenith) torso clique
5. Which of the following has a torso? guidebook spider (human being)

Read each set of words below. Cross out the one word in each group that is not a synonym.

6. gang group sound clique
7. pinnacle top zenith loss
8. instrument loot rob ransack
9. argue bicker slot fight
10. tariff tax delay duty

page 86

Have No Fear

Don't worry—algebra is nothing to fear! But some people do fear specific things, like heights, snakes, or fire. These strong fears are called phobias.

To find out what each phobia below means, use the distributive property to simplify each expression. Draw a line to match the expression to its simplest form.

1. Zoophobia $4n + 2n$ → $6n + 36$ Fear of Water
2. Nyctophobia $x + 3x$ → $6n + 3$ Fear of Snakes
3. Astraphobia $p + 8 + 7p$ → $8x + 28$ Fear of Light
4. Ophidiophobia $8n + 3 - 2n$ → $6n$ Fear of Animals
5. Pyrophobia $4(x + 3)$ → $9n + 12$ Fear of Dirt
6. Acrophobia $6p + 17 - 8 - 2p$ → $12p + 30$ Fear of Infinity
7. Hydrophobia $3(n + 6) + 3(n + 6)$ → $4p + 9$ Fear of Heights
8. Photophobia $7(2x + 4) - 6x$ → $4x + 12$ Fear of Fire
9. Apeirophobia $5(2p + 6) + 2$ → $4x$ Fear of Darkness
10. Mysophobia $n(6 + 3) + 12$ → $8p + 8$ Fear of Lightning

page 87

Writing to a Prompt

Do you dream of the beach or the mountains when you think of a perfect vacation? Perhaps you cannot decide between the two but can think of a perfect spot where the two come together. Even if you have never visited your dream location, you have seen pictures and/or videos that make you long to go there.
Choose a location. Describe the scenery. How does it look? What feelings does the place evoke? What are the smells and sounds that are unique to your special place?
Describe this special place in as much detail as possible so that the reader can be transported there in their mind's eye.

A Dream Vacation

Answers will vary.

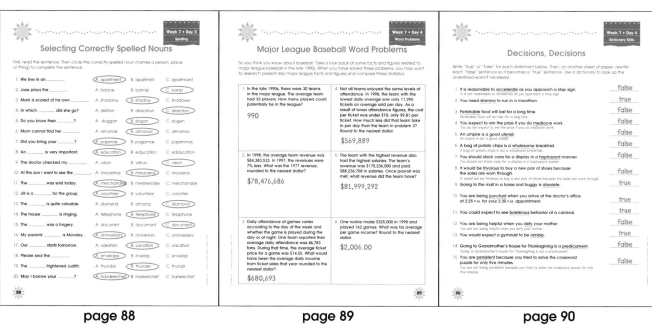

page 88

Selecting Correctly Spelled Nouns

First, read the sentence. Then circle the correctly spelled noun (names a person, place, or thing) to complete the sentence.

1. We live in an _____. **(A. apartment)** B. apartmint C. apartmant
2. Jose plays the _____. A. banjoe B. banijo **(C. banjo)**
3. Mark is scared of his own _____. A. shaddow **(B. shadow)** C. shadowe
4. In which _____ did she go? A. dirktion B. direcshun **(C. direction)**
5. Do you know their _____? A. sloggan **(B. slogan)** C. slogen
6. Mom cannot find her _____. A. almanak **(B. almanac)** C. allmanac
7. Did you bring your _____? **(A. pajamas)** B. pagamas C. pajammas
8. An _____ is very important. **(A. education)** B. edducation C. edducation
9. The doctor checked my _____. A. vizion B. vishun **(C. vision)**
10. At the zoo I want to see the _____. A. rinocerus **(B. rhinoceros)** C. rinoceros
11. The _____ was sold today. **(A. merchandise)** B. mershendise C. merchandize
12. Jill is a _____ for the group. **(A. volunteer)** B. voluntear C. volunter
13. The _____ is quite valuable. A. diamend **(B. diamond)** C. dimond
14. The house _____ is ringing. A. tellephone **(B. telephone)** C. telaphone
15. The _____ was a forgery. A. documint B. documant **(C. document)**
16. My parents' _____ is Monday. **(A. anniversary)** B. anniversry C. anniversery
17. Our _____ starts tomorrow. A. vakation **(B. vacation)** C. vacatiun
18. Please seal the _____. **(A. envelope)** B. invelop C. envelop
19. The _____ frightened Judith. A. thundar **(B. thunder)** C. thundir
20. May I borrow your _____? **(A. handkerchief)** B. hankerchief C. hankerchef

---

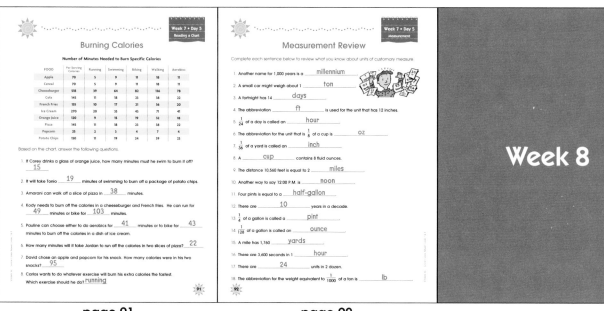

page 89

Major League Baseball Word Problems

So you think you know about baseball? Take a look back at some facts and figures related to major league baseball in the late 1990s. When you have solved these problems, you may want to research present-day major league facts and figures and compare these statistics.

1. In the late 1990s, there were 30 teams in the major league. The average team had 33 players. How many players could potentially be in the league?
990

2. In 1998, the average team revenue was $84,383,533. In 1997, the revenues were 7% less. What was the 1997 revenue, rounded to the nearest dollar?
$78,476,686

3. Daily attendance at games varies according to the day of the week and whether the game is played during the day or at night. One team reported their average daily attendance was 46,783 fans. During that time, the average ticket price for a game was $14.55. What would have been the average daily income from ticket sales that year rounded to the nearest dollar?
$680,693

4. Not all teams enjoyed the same levels of attendance. In 1998, the team with the lowest daily average saw only 11,295 tickets on average sold per day. As a result of lower attendance figures, the cost per ticket was under $10, only $9.81 per ticket. How much less did that team take in per day than the team in problem 3? Round to the nearest dollar.
$569,889

5. The team with the highest revenue also had the highest salaries. The team's revenue was $170,236,000 and paid $88,236,708 in salaries. Once payroll was met, what revenue did the team have?
$81,999,292

6. One rookie made $325,000 in 1998 and played 162 games. What was his average per game income? Round to the nearest dollar.
$2,006.00

---

page 90

Decisions, Decisions

Write "true" or "false" for each statement below. Then, on another sheet of paper, rewrite each "false" sentence so it becomes a "true" sentence. Use a dictionary to look up the underlined word if necessary.

1. It is reasonable to accelerate as you approach a stop sign. — **false**
2. You need stamina to run in a marathon. — **true**
3. Perishable food will last for a long time. — **false**
4. You expect to win the prize if you do mediocre work. — **false**
5. An umpire is a good utensil. — **false**
6. A bag of potato chips is a wholesome breakfast. — **false**
7. You should stack cans for a display in a haphazard manner. — **false**
8. It would be frivolous to buy a new pair of shoes because the soles are worn through. — **false**
9. Going to the mall in a horse and buggy is obsolete. — **true**
10. You are being punctual when you arrive at the doctor's office at 2:25 P.M. for your 2:30 P.M. appointment. — **true**
11. You could expect to see boisterous behavior at a carnival. — **true**
12. You are being helpful when you defy your mother. — **false**
13. You would expect a gymnast to be nimble. — **true**
14. Going to Grandmother's house for Thanksgiving is a predicament. — **false**
15. You are persistent because you tried to solve the crossword puzzle for only five minutes. — **false**

---

page 91

Burning Calories

Number of Minutes Needed to Burn Specific Calories

FOOD	Per Serving Calories	Running	Swimming	Biking	Walking	Aerobics
Apple	70	5	9	11	18	11
Cereal	70	5	9	11	18	11
Cheeseburger	518	39	64	82	136	78
Cola	145	11	18	23	38	22
French Fries	135	10	17	21	36	20
Ice Cream	270	20	33	43	71	41
Orange Juice	120	9	15	19	32	18
Pizza	145	11	18	23	38	22
Popcorn	25	2	3	4	7	4
Potato Chips	150	11	19	24	39	23

Based on the chart, answer the following questions.

1. If Corey drinks a glass of orange juice, how many minutes must he swim to burn it off? **15**
2. It will take Tonio **19** minutes of swimming to burn off a package of potato chips.
3. Amarani can walk off a slice of pizza in **38** minutes.
4. Kody needs to burn off the calories in a cheeseburger and French fries. He can run for **49** minutes or bike for **103** minutes.
5. Pauline can choose either to do aerobics for **41** minutes or to bike for **43** minutes to burn off the calories in a dish of ice cream.
6. How many minutes will it take Jordan to run off the calories in two slices of pizza? **22**
7. David chose an apple and popcorn for his snack. How many calories were in his two snacks? **95**
8. Carlos wants to do whatever exercise will burn his extra calories the fastest. Which exercise should he do? **running**

---

page 92

Measurement Review

Complete each sentence below to review what you know about units of customary measure.

1. Another name for 1,000 years is a **millennium**.
2. A small car might weigh about 1 **ton**.
3. A fortnight has 14 **days**.
4. The abbreviation **ft** is used for the unit that has 12 inches.
5. $\frac{1}{24}$ of a day is called an **hour**.
6. The abbreviation for the unit that is $\frac{1}{8}$ of a cup is **oz**.
7. $\frac{1}{36}$ of a yard is called an **inch**.
8. A **cup** contains 8 fluid ounces.
9. The distance 10,560 feet is equal to 2 **miles**.
10. Another way to say 12:00 P.M. is **noon**.
11. Four pints is equal to a **half-gallon**.
12. There are **10** years in a decade.
13. $\frac{1}{4}$ of a gallon is called a **pint**.
14. $\frac{1}{128}$ of a gallon is called an **ounce**.
15. A mile has 1,760 **yards**.
16. There are 3,600 seconds in 1 **hour**.
17. There are **24** units in 2 dozen.
18. The abbreviation for the weight equivalent to $\frac{1}{1000}$ of a ton is **lb**.

Week 8

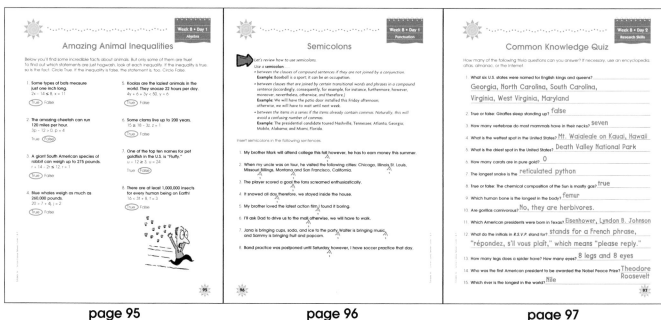

page 95

Amazing Animal Inequalities

Below you'll find some incredible facts about animals. But only some of them are true! To find out which statements are just hogwash, look at each inequality. If the inequality is true, so is the fact. Circle True. If the inequality is false, the statement is, too. Circle False.

1. Some types of bats measure just one inch long.
$2x - 14 \leq 8, x = 11$
True False

2. The amazing cheetah can run 120 miles per hour.
$3p - 12 > 0, p = 4$
True **False**

3. A giant South American species of rabbit can weigh up to 275 pounds.
$r + 14 - 2r \leq 12, r = 1$
True False

4. Blue whales weigh as much as 260,000 pounds.
$20 > 7 \times 4, j = 2$
True False

5. Koalas are the laziest animals in the world. They snooze 22 hours per day.
$4y + 6 + 3y < 50, y = 6$
True False

6. Some clams live up to 200 years.
$15 \geq 18 - 3z, z = 1$
True False

7. One of the top ten names for pet goldfish in the U.S. is "Fluffy."
$u - 12 \geq 3, u = 24$
True **False**

8. There are at least 1,000,000 insects for every human being on Earth!
$16 < 3t + 8, t = 3$
True False

---

page 96

Semicolons

Let's review how to use semicolons.
Use a **semicolon**:
- between the clauses of compound sentences if they are not joined by a conjunction.
  Example: Baseball is a sport; it can be an occupation.
- between clauses that are joined by certain transitional words and phrases in a compound sentence (accordingly, consequently, for example, for instance, furthermore, however, moreover, nevertheless, otherwise, and therefore.)
  Example: We will have the patio door installed this Friday afternoon; otherwise, we will have to wait until next week.
- between the items in a series if the items already contain commas. Naturally, this will avoid a confusing number of commas.
  Example: The presidential candidate toured Nashville, Tennessee; Atlanta, Georgia; Mobile, Alabama; and Miami, Florida.

Insert semicolons in the following sentences.

1. My brother Mark will attend college this fall however, he has to earn money this summer.
2. When my uncle was on tour, he visited the following cities: Chicago, Illinois St. Louis, Missouri Billings, Montana and San Francisco, California.
3. The player scored a goal the fans screamed enthusiastically.
4. It snowed all day therefore, we stayed inside the house.
5. My brother loved the latest action film I found it boring.
6. I'll ask Dad to drive us to the mall otherwise, we will have to walk.
7. Jana is bringing cups, soda, and ice to the party Walter is bringing music, and Sammy is bringing fruit and popcorn.
8. Band practice was postponed until Saturday however, I have soccer practice that day.

---

page 97

Common Knowledge Quiz

How many of these trivia questions can you answer? If necessary, use an encyclopedia, atlas, almanac, or the Internet.

1. What six U.S. states were named for English kings and queens? **Georgia, North Carolina, South Carolina, Virginia, West Virginia, Maryland**
2. True or false: Giraffes sleep standing up? **false**
3. How many vertebrae do most mammals have in their necks? **seven**
4. What is the wettest spot in the United States? **Mt. Waialeale on Kauai, Hawaii**
5. What is the driest spot in the United States? **Death Valley National Park**
6. How many carats are in pure gold? **0**
7. The longest snake is the **reticulated python**
8. True or false: The chemical composition of the Sun is mostly gas? **true**
9. Which human bone is the longest in the body? **femur**
10. Are gorillas carnivorous? **No, they are herbivores.**
11. Which American presidents were born in Texas? **Eisenhower, Lyndon B. Johnson**
12. What do the initials in R.S.V.P. stand for? **stands for a French phrase, "répondez, s'il vous plaît," which means "please reply."**
13. How many legs does a spider have? How many eyes? **8 legs and 8 eyes**
14. Who was the first American president to be awarded the Nobel Peace Prize? **Theodore Roosevelt**
15. Which river is the longest in the world? **Nile**

Week 8 • Day 2
Analogies

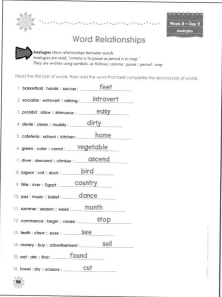

Word Relationships

Analogies *show relationships between words.*
Analogies are read, "comma is to pause as period is to stop."
They are written using symbols, as follows: comma : pause :: period : stop

Read the first pair of words; then add the word that best completes the second pair of words.

1. basketball : hands :: soccer : feet
2. sociable : extrovert :: retiring : introvert
3. prohibit : allow :: strenuous : easy
4. sterile : clean :: muddy : dirty
5. cafeteria : school :: kitchen : home
6. green : color :: carrot : vegetable
7. diver : descend :: climber : ascend
8. jaguar : cat :: duck : bird
9. Nile : river :: Egypt : country
10. jazz : music :: ballet : dance
11. summer : season :: week : month
12. commence : begin :: cease : stop
13. teeth : chew :: eyes : see
14. money : buy :: advertisement : sell
15. eat : ate :: find : found
16. towel : dry :: scissors : cut

98

page 98

Week 8 • Day 3
Subject-Verb Agreement

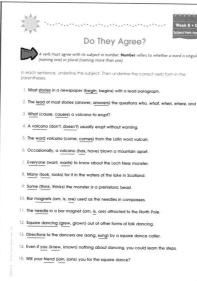

Do They Agree?

A verb must agree with its subject in number. **Number** *refers to whether a word is singular (naming one) or plural (naming more than one).*

In each sentence, underline the subject. Then underline the correct verb form in the parentheses.

1. Most stories in a newspaper (begin, begins) with a lead paragraph.
2. The lead of most stories (answer, answers) the questions *who, what, when, where,* and *why.*
3. What (cause, causes) a volcano to erupt?
4. A volcano (don't, doesn't) usually erupt without warning.
5. The word *volcano* (come, comes) from the Latin word *vulcan.*
6. Occasionally, a volcano (has, have) blown a mountain apart.
7. Everyone (want, wants) to know about the Loch Ness monster.
8. Many (look, looks) for it in the waters of the lake in Scotland.
9. Some (think, thinks) the monster is a prehistoric beast.
10. Bar magnets (am, is, are) used as the needles in compasses.
11. The needle in a bar magnet (am, is, are) attracted to the North Pole.
12. Square dancing (grew, grown) out of other forms of folk dancing.
13. Directions to the dancers are (sang, sung) by a square dance caller.
14. Even if you (knew, known) nothing about dancing, you could learn the steps.
15. Will your friend (join, joins) you for the square dance?

99

page 99

Week 8 • Day 3
Algebra

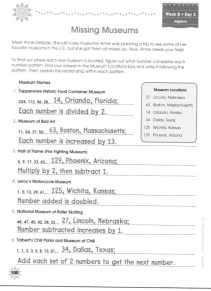

Missing Museums

Meet Anne DeSplay. She just loves museums! Anne was planning a trip to see some of her favorite museums in the U.S., but she got them all mixed up. Now, Anne needs your help!

To find out where each real museum is located, figure out what number completes each number pattern. Find your answer in the Museum Locations box and write it following the pattern. Then, explain the relationship within each pattern.

Museum Locations
27 Lincoln, Nebraska
63 Boston, Massachusetts
14 Orlando, Florida
34 Dallas, Texas
125 Wichita, Kansas
129 Phoenix, Arizona

Museum Names

1. Tupperware Historic Food Container Museum
   224, 112, 56, 28,... 14, Orlando, Florida;
   Each number is divided by 2.
2. Museum of Bad Art
   11, 24, 37, 50,... 63, Boston, Massachusetts;
   Each number is increased by 13.
3. Hall of Flame (Fire Fighting Museum)
   5, 9, 17, 33, 65,... 129, Phoenix, Arizona;
   Multiply by 2, then subtract 1.
4. Leroy's Motorcycle Museum
   1, 5, 13, 29, 61,... 125, Wichita, Kansas;
   Number added is doubled.
5. National Museum of Roller Skating
   48, 47, 45, 42, 38, 33,... 27, Lincoln, Nebraska;
   Number subtracted increases by 1.
6. Tolbert's Chili Parlor and Museum of Chili
   1, 1, 2, 3, 5, 8, 13, 21,... 34, Dallas, Texas;
   Add each set of 2 numbers to get the next number.

100

page 100

Week 8 • Day 4
Business Letter

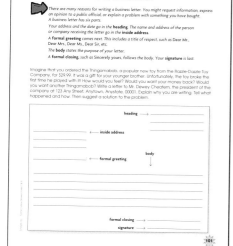

It's All Business

There are many reasons for writing a business letter. You might request information, express an opinion to a public official, or explain a problem with something you have bought. A business letter has six parts.

Your address and the date go in the **heading**. *The name and address of the person or company receiving the letter go in the* **inside address**.

A **formal greeting** *comes next. This includes a title of respect, such as* Dear Mr., Dear Mrs., Dear Ms., Dear Sir, etc.

The **body** *states the purpose of your letter.*

A **formal closing,** *such as* Sincerely yours, *follows the body. Your* **signature** *is last.*

Imagine that you ordered the Thingamabob, a popular new toy from the Razzle-Dazzle Toy Company, for $29.99. It was a gift for your younger brother. Unfortunately, the toy broke the first time he played with it! How would you feel? Would you want your money back? Would you want another Thingamabob? Write a letter to Mr. Dewey Cheatem, the president of the company at 123 Any Street, Anytown, Anystate, 00001. Explain why you are writing. Tell what happened and how. Then suggest a solution to the problem.

heading →
← inside address
← formal greeting
body ↓
formal closing →
signature →

101

page 101

Week 8 • Day 4
Reading Comprehension

Strange New World

Amira opened her eyes. It wasn't a dream. A moment ago she was in her bland living room with her friend Cesar, playing an old video game. Now that bland room was gone.

She and Cesar stood in a crudely rendered world of primary colors. Everything looked blocky, like it was made of large colored bricks. There were green blocks underfoot, blue and white blocks in the sky. A blocky turtle waddled past them. Suddenly, she realized, *they are all made of pixels!* Cesar laughed.

He took off, sprinting down the blocky green path. Amira had to dash to keep up with him. He stopped so suddenly that she almost ran into him. Before she could catch her breath, he pointed up at what had caught his eye.

It was a big yellow block, as tall as either of them, inexplicably **suspended** in the air about ten feet above them. They could see no wires.

Before she could stop him, Cesar leapt up into the air. This new world had granted them new abilities, too, because he flew up three times the height he normally could and head-butted the floating block.

CLINK! A giant coin shot out of the top of the block. Amira tried to move out of the way, but the coin was plummeting toward her. She cringed. As soon as it touched her, the coin faded harmlessly. She exhaled softly.

Cesar pointed down the path where more yellow blocks waited in a row. He held out his hand. Amira looked from his outstretched hand to the blocky path ahead, then back at his beaming face. She took a deep breath. She smiled, reached out, and took his hand.

Answer the following questions.

1. This story takes place—
   A. on Mars.
   B. at a barbecue.
   C. in a living room.
   (D) in a video game.
2. First, Amira—
   A. opens her eyes.
   B. takes Cesar's hand.
   C. smiled.
   (D) plays a video game.
3. CLINK! is an example of the literary term—
   (A) onomatopoeia.
   B. alliteration.
   C. allusion.
   D. foreshadowing.
4. Suspended is used in this story to mean—
   (A.) to hang in midair.
   B. to sprint down the path.
   C. to be temporarily forced to leave school.
   D. to spur to action.
5. When Cesar sees the ______, he ______
   A. blocky turtle; catches it.
   B. giant coin; runs away.
   (C.) big yellow block; head-butts it.
   D. green blocky path; collapses.
6. The blocks making up the world are—
   A. coins.
   (B.) pixels.
   C. atoms.
   D. friends.

102

page 102

Week 8 • Day 5
Problem Solving

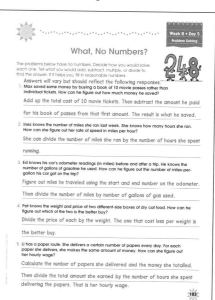

What, No Numbers?

The problems below have no numbers. Decide how you would solve each one. Tell what you would add, subtract, multiply, or divide to find the answer. If it helps you, fill in reasonable numbers.

Answers will vary but should reflect the following responses.

1. Max saved some money by buying a book of 10 movie passes rather than individual tickets. How can he figure out how much money he saved?
   Add up the total cost of 10 movie tickets. Then subtract the amount he paid for his book of passes from that first amount. The result is what he saved.
2. Inez knows the number of miles she ran last week. She knows how many hours she ran. How can she figure out her rate of speed in miles per hour?
   She can divide the number of miles she ran by the number of hours she spent running.
3. Ed knows his car's odometer readings (in miles) before and after a trip. He knows the number of gallons of gasoline he used. How can he figure out the number of miles-per-gallon his car got on the trip?
   Figure out miles he traveled using the start and end number on the odometer. Then divide the number of miles by number of gallons of gas used.
4. Pat knows the weight and price of two different-size boxes of dry cat food. How can he figure out which of the two is the better buy?
   Divide the price of each by the weight. The one that cost less per weight is the better buy.
5. Li has a paper route. She delivers a certain number of papers every day. For each paper she delivers, she makes the same amount of money. How can she figure out her hourly wage?
   Calculate the number of papers she delivered and the money she totalled. Then divide the total amount she earned by the number of hours she spent delivering the papers. That is her hourly wage.

103

page 103

Week 8 • Day 5
Reading for Details

Forests on Fire

Winds blow over the dry Mojave Desert and travel toward the Pacific Ocean.

There are some places where you can expect wildfires. In California, fires burn 50,000 to 500,000 acres of land every year. Some of the plants that live there have oily sap. They can survive the dry, hot summers, but if they catch fire they explode into flame. Grasses grow thick during the spring rains and then die. They dry into a thick layer of straw that burns fast, making a very hot fire.

Fires can start wherever there's fuel to burn. Southern California has plenty of fuel and a hot, dry wind that blows every year between mid-September and late October. This wind, called the Santa Ana, passes over the inland desert, losing moisture and gaining heat, and rushes toward the ocean to the west. The Santa Ana wind fans the flames and makes fighting the fires nearly impossible.

Forests are a natural storehouse of fuel for a fire. During a dry summer, dead trees and low brush in a forest can burst into flame wherever lightning strikes. Rain usually puts out these fires. But sometimes the combination of dry fuel, hot dry air, and strong winds is just right for a major forest fire.

In 1988, Wyoming's Yellowstone National Park was burned by several such fires at once. Lightning struck in two places. A worker dropped a lit cigarette in another place. On the worst day of the fire, more than 600 square kilometers (about 230 square miles) of forest burned. Clouds of smoke that looked like storm clouds rose into the atmosphere. Smoke blocked the sun and drifted far beyond the park.

Firefighters work hard to control fires like those in Yellowstone and California, many of which are caused by people. But long before humans learned how to start or put out a fire, prairies and forests burned every year. Both kinds of land recovered, as they have in Yellowstone and in California.

1. What mountains are between Los Angeles and the Mojave Desert? The Santa Monica Mtns.
2. What path do the Santa Ana winds follow? from inland desert out to sea
3. Why might a rainy spring increase the risk of forest fires?
   growth of fuel; grasses grow thick in spring rains, then dry over summer.
4. In 1988, what caused the fires in Yellowstone National Park?
   lightning and a cigarette
5. True or false: Yellowstone is located in California: false

104

page 104

Week 9

Week 9 • Day 1
Logic

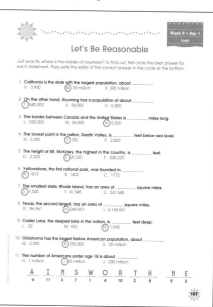

Let's Be Reasonable

Just exactly where is the middle of nowhere? To find out, first circle the best answer for each statement. Then write the letter of the correct answer in the code at the bottom.

1. California is the state with the largest population, about ______.
   V. 3,900 — (W.) 39 million — X. 390 million
2. On the other hand, Wyoming has a population of about ______.
   (T.) 540,000 — U. 54,000 — V. 5,400
3. The border between Canada and the United States is ______ miles long.
   L. 550,000 — M. 55,000 — (N.) 5,500
4. The lowest point in the nation, Death Valley, is ______ feet below sea level.
   N. 0.282 — (O.) 282 — P. 2,820
5. The height of Mt. McKinley, the highest in the country, is ______ feet.
   D. 2,320 — (E.) 20,320 — F. 200,320
6. Yellowstone, the first national park, was founded in ______.
   (A.) 1872 — B. 1802 — C. 1772
7. The smallest state, Rhode Island, has an area of ______ square miles.
   (S.) 1,545 — T. 41,545 — U. 241,545
8. Texas, the second largest, has an area of ______ square miles.
   G. 86,861 — (H.) 268,601 — I. 6,168,601
9. Crater Lake, the deepest lake in the nation, is ______ feet deep.
   L. 32 — M. 932 — (N.) 1,943
10. Oklahoma has the largest Native American population, about ______.
    Q. 2,500 — (R.) 250,000 — S. 25 million
11. The number of Americans under age 18 is about ______.
    H. 1 million — (I.) 65 million — J. 200 million

A	I	N	S	W	O	R	T	H,	N	E
6	11	3	7	1	4	10	2	8	9	5

107

page 107

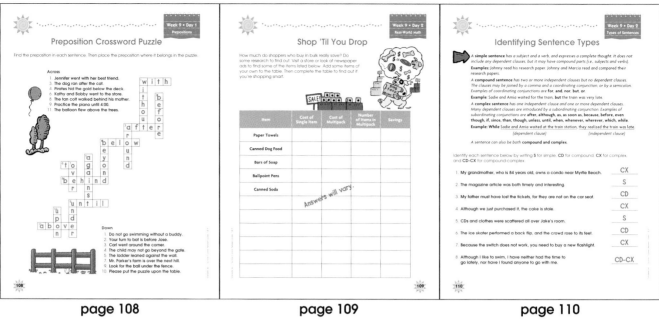

page 108

Preposition Crossword Puzzle

Find the preposition in each sentence. Then place the preposition where it belongs in the puzzle.

Across
1. Jennifer went with her best friend.
2. The dog ran after the cat.
3. Pirates hid the gold below the deck.
4. Kathy and Bobby went to the store.
5. The tan colt walked behind his mother.
9. Practice the piano until 4:00.
11. The balloon flew above the trees.

Down
1. Do not go swimming without a buddy.
2. Your turn to bat is before Jose.
3. Carl went around the corner.
4. The child may not go beyond the gate.
5. The ladder leaned against the wall.
6. Mr. Parker's farm is over the next hill.
7. Look for the ball under the fence.
10. Please put the puzzle upon the table.

Puzzle answers: with, without, before, after, below, around, to, over, against, behind, beyond, until, upon, under, above

page 109

Shop 'Til You Drop

How much do shoppers who buy in bulk really save? Do some research to find out. Visit a store or look at newspaper ads to find some of the items listed below. Add some items of your own to the table. Then complete the table to find out if you're shopping smart.

Item	Cost of Single Item	Cost of Multipack	Number of Items in Multipack	Savings
Paper Towels				
Canned Dog Food				
Bars of Soap				
Ballpoint Pens				
Canned Soda				

Answers will vary.

page 110

Identifying Sentence Types

A **simple sentence** has a subject and a verb, and expresses a complete thought. It does not include any dependent clauses, but it may have compound parts (i.e., subjects and verbs).
Examples: Johnny read his research paper. Johnny and Marcia read and compared their research papers.

A **compound sentence** has two or more independent clauses but no dependent clauses. The clauses may be joined by a comma and a coordinating conjunction, or by a semicolon. Examples of coordinating conjunctions are **for, and, nor, but, or.**
Example: Sadie and Amia waited for the train, but the train was very late.

A **complex sentence** has one independent clause and one or more dependent clauses. Many dependent clauses are introduced by a subordinating conjunction. Examples of subordinating conjunctions are **after, although, as, as soon as, because, before, even though, if, since, than, though, unless, until, when, whenever, wherever, which, while.**
Example: While Sadie and Amia waited at the train station, they realized the train was late.
(dependent clause) *(independent clause)*

A sentence can also be both **compound and complex.**

Identify each sentence below by writing **S** for simple, **CD** for compound, **CX** for complex, and **CD-CX** for compound-complex.

1. My grandmother, who is 84 years old, owns a condo near Myrtle Beach. — **CX**
2. The magazine article was both timely and interesting. — **S**
3. My father must have lost the tickets, for they are not on the car seat. — **CD**
4. Although we just purchased it, the cake is stale. — **CX**
5. CDs and clothes were scattered all over Jake's room. — **S**
6. The ice skater performed a back flip, and the crowd rose to its feet. — **CD**
7. Because the switch does not work, you need to buy a new flashlight. — **CX**
8. Although I like to swim, I have neither had the time to go lately, nor have I found anyone to go with me. — **CD-CX**

page 111

Math Puzzles and Tricks

Solve the following math puzzles and tricks.

1. On June 9 of this year, Walt Disney Studio created Donald Duck. To find the year:
   • The tens and unit digits are consecutive integers whose sum is 7 and product is 12.
   • The tens digit is ⅓ of the hundreds digit.
   • The sum of all the digits is 17.
   Donald Duck was created in **1934** (year).

2. To do this trick, you will need a calculator.
   • First, enter the number 37037.
   • Next, multiply your favorite digit from 1 to 9 by 3 (Do this step in your head.)
   • Then, multiply the number in the calculator by the above answer (the number in your head.)
   • Finally, you should end with a row of 6 of your favorite numbers.
   What is it? **Answers will vary.**

3. Astronaut Neil Armstrong became the first person to step on the moon. His famous quote is "That's one small step for a man, one giant leap for mankind." To find the year:
   • The tens digit is a perfect number.
   • The hundreds and units digits are the same square number.
   • The sum of all the digits is 25.
   Neil Armstrong walked on the moon in **1969**.

4. A two-hundred pound man and his two sons, each of whom weigh one hundred pounds, want to cross a river. They have only one boat that can only carry two hundred pounds.
   How will they all cross the river? **The two sons row across. One stays while the other rows back. That son then stays while the father rows back again by himself. The son originally dropped off then rows over and brings back the other son.**

5. Write your house number, double it, add 5, multiply by 50, add your age, subtract 615. The answer will contain both your house number and your age.
   Answers will vary.

6. You are the pilot of an airplane that flies from New York to Chicago, a distance of 1,000 miles. The plane's air speed averages 200 miles per hour and makes one 30 minute stop.
   What is the pilot's name? **my name**

page 112

Alberto Santos Dumont: Brazil's Favorite Aviator

Most people have heard of the Wright Brothers, the two Americans generally considered the inventors of the first practical airplane. Few people other than Brazilians (and certain aviation enthusiasts) have heard of Alberto Santos Dumont, another visionary in early aviation.

Santos Dumont was born in 1873 in Minas Gerais, Brazil. When he turned 18, he was sent to Paris to study chemistry, astronomy, and mechanics. While in Paris, he became interested in **dirigibles**, or airships held up by a "lighter-than-air" gas often contained in a balloon.

Santos Dumont's balloons won many races and prizes, including one in 1901 for circling the Eiffel Tower in less than 30 minutes. Reportedly, Santos Dumont took the 100,000 franc prize and split it among his workers and Paris's beggars.

After conquering the skies in lighter-than-air vehicles, Santos Dumont became interested in heavier-than-air vehicles. His 14-BIS plane left the ground on November 12, 1906, to fly at a speed of approximately 37 km/h and a height of 6 meters to reach a total distance of 220 meters. This flight won him the Archdeacon Prize and demonstrated that a heavier-than-air vehicle could take off by its own means.

The Wright Brothers had flown their *Flyer I* in 1903 with the help of a catapult's launch. The Wright Flyer, once airborne, flew for longer distances at a higher altitude than the 14-BIS. Therefore, most people consider the Wright Flyer the first practical airplane. Undaunted by this classification, Brazilians still celebrate Santos Dumont as a national hero.

Answer the following questions.

1. Alberto Santos Dumont was—
   A. a Wright brother.
   B. the developer of the *Flyer I.*
   C. an aviator and inventor.
   D. never celebrated in his birth country.

2. Aviation's Latin root is avis, which probably means—
   A. brick.
   B. bird.
   C. Brazilian.
   D. winner.

3. A synonym for aviator is most likely—
   A. enthusiast.
   B. beggar.
   C. winner.
   D. pilot.

4. What happened first?
   A. The Wright Brothers flew *Flyer I.*
   B. Santos Dumont flew the 14-BIS.
   C. Santos Dumont won 100,000 francs.
   D. Santos Dumont won the Archdeacon.

5. The difference between a dirigible and an airplane is—
   A. one is lighter-than-air and one is heavier-than-air.
   B. dirigibles are more popular today.
   C. airplanes were invented first.
   D. there is no difference.

6. Because Santos Dumont won the race—
   A. he received the 100,000 franc prize.
   B. he gave his proceeds to charity.
   C. he built the 14-BIS.
   D. he is a Brazilian national hero.

page 113

Mean, Mode, Median & Range

Mean, median, and **mode** are three kinds of averages. **Range** is the difference between the largest and smallest value in the group of numbers.
1) To find the **mean** of a set of numbers, add all the numbers and then divide their sum by the number of addends.
2) The middle number in a set of numbers is the **median.** To find the **median,** the numbers must first be arranged in order. If there are two middle numbers (which will occur if there is an even number of addends), the **median** is the average of the two middle numbers.
3) **Mode** refers to the number that occurs most frequently in a set of data.

Find the mean, mode, median, and range for each data set.

1. Erik planted ten apple trees. He kept track of how many apples he picked from each tree. His results are shown in the table:

Tree #	1	2	3	4	5	6	7	8	9	10
# of Apples	137	120	140	141	137	124	119	129	137	136

Mean: **132**   Median: **136.5**   Mode: **137**   Range: **22**

2. Over the summer, Tamara read four mystery novels. The table shows how many pages each book had:

Book Title	An Eye for Mystery	Unbelievable!	The Treehouse Nextdoor	Treading Lightly
# of Pages	512	272	368	512

Mean: **416**   Median: **320**   Mode: **512**   Range: **240**

3. Seven friends have a contest to see how long they can balance their left foot. Their results are shown in the table:

Name	Adeela	Henry	Wendy	Kenny	Thea	Winston	Cyrus
Time (seconds)	56	35	88	65	91.6	35	63.4

Mean: **62**   Median: **63.4**   Mode: **35**   Range: **56.6**

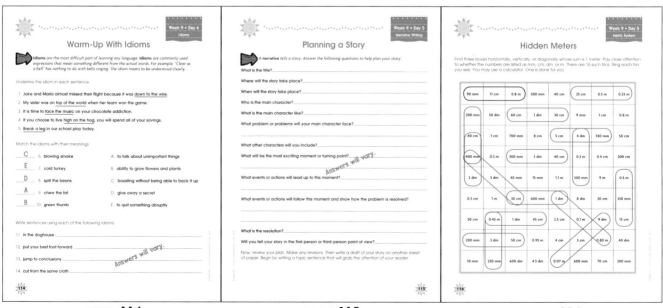

page 114

Warm-Up With Idioms

Idioms are the most difficult part of learning any language. **Idioms** are commonly used expressions that mean something different from the actual words. For example, "Clear as a bell" has nothing to do with bells ringing. The idiom means to be understood clearly.

Underline the idiom in each sentence.

1. Jake and Maria almost missed their flight because it was **down to the wire.**
2. My sister was **on top of the world** when her team won the game.
3. It is time to **face the music** on your chocolate addiction.
4. If you choose to live **high on the hog,** you will spend all of your savings.
5. **Break a leg** in our school play today.

Match the idioms with their meanings.

C 6. blowing smoke — A. to talk about unimportant things
E 7. cold turkey — B. ability to grow flowers and plants
D 8. spill the beans — C. boasting without being able to back it up
A 9. chew the fat — D. give away a secret
B 10. green thumb — E. to quit something abruptly

Write sentences using each of the following idioms.

11. in the doghouse
12. put your best foot forward
13. jump to conclusions
14. cut from the same cloth

Answers will vary.

page 115

Planning a Story

A **narrative** tells a story. Answer the following questions to help plan your story.

What is the title?
Where will the story take place?
When will the story take place?
Who is the main character?
What is the main character like?
What problem or problems will your main character face?
What other characters will you include?
What will be the most exciting moment or turning point?
What events or actions will lead up to this moment?
What events or actions will follow this moment and show how the problem is resolved?
What is the resolution?
Will you tell your story in the first-person or third-person point of view?

Now, review your plan. Make any revisions. Then write a draft of your story on another sheet of paper. Begin by writing a topic sentence that will grab the attention of your reader.

Answers will vary.

page 116

Hidden Meters

Find three boxes horizontally, vertically, or diagonally whose sum is 1 meter. Pay close attention to whether the numbers are listed as mm, cm, dm, or m. There are 16 such trios you see. You may use a calculator. One is done for you.

90 mm	11 cm	0.8 m	500 mm	40 cm	25 cm	0.5 m	0.25 m
200 mm	50 dm	60 cm	1 dm	30 cm	9 mm	1 cm	0.8 m
40 cm	1 cm	700 mm	8 cm	5 cm	4 dm	550 mm	50 cm
400 mm	0.3 m	300 mm	3 dm	40 cm	0.3 m	0.4 cm	300 cm
2 dm	3 dm	40 mm	15 mm	1.1 m	300 mm	9 m	0.5 m
0.3 cm	1 m	30 cm	600 mm	1 dm	8 cm	20 cm	350 mm
50 cm	0.45 m	1 dm	45 cm	2.5 cm	0.1 m	9 dm	15 cm
200 mm	3 dm	0.3 m	0.95 cm	3 cm	3 cm	0.80 m	40 cm
10 mm	250 mm	600 dm	4.5 dm	0.07 m	600 mm	70 cm	300 mm

Week 10

---

page 119

Stumpers

Write your answers in both number and word form, for example, 14.37 (number form), fourteen and thirty-seven hundredths (word form).

1. Who Am I?
A. I have 4 digits and they are all different.
B. All of my digits are odd.
C. I have a 1 in the hundredths place.
D. I have a 7 in the ones place.
E. The number in the tens place is less than the number in the tenths place.
F. None of my digits is 9.

Answer: 37.51

thirty-seven and fifty-one hundredths

2. Who Am I?
A. I have 4 digits, and they are all odd.
B. The number in the tenths place is greater than 3. It is a factor of 36.
C. The number in the hundredths place is less than 4 and greater than 1.
D. The numbers in the ones and tens places are the same and are also factors of 25.

Answer: 55.93

fifty-five and ninety-three hundredths

3. Who Am I?
A. I have 4 digits, and they are all different and even.
B. The number in the hundredths place is half of the number in the tenths place.
C. The number in the hundredths place is greater than 3.
D. The number in the ones place is 6.
E. The number in the tens place is 2.

Answer: 26.84

twenty-six and eighty-four hundredths

4. Who Am I?
A. I have 4 digits.
B. Each digit is either a 2 or a 4.
C. The numbers in the ones place and tenths place are the same.
D. The numbers in the tens place and hundredths place are the same.
E. I have a 4 in the hundredths place.

Answer: 42.24

forty-two and twenty-four hundredths

5. Who Am I?
A. I have 3 even digits.
B. The number in the tenths place when subtracted from 3 equals 1.
C. The number in the ones place is 8.
D. Divide the number in the ones place by 2 and you will have the number in the hundredths place.

Answer: 8.24

eight and twenty-four hundredths

6. Who Am I?
A. I have 4 digits, and they are all odd.
B. The 2-digit whole number is greater than 10 and less than 20. When this number is divided into 121, the quotient is also that number.
C. The digit in the tenths place is 3.
D. Add 4 to the number in the tens place and you will have the number in the hundredths place.

Answer: 11.37

eleven and thirty-seven hundredths

---

page 120

Adverbs That Compare

Adverbs can be used to compare actions. A **comparative adverb**, which compares two actions, ends in -er or begins with *more* or *less*. A **superlative adverb**, which compares more than two actions, ends in -est or begins with *most* or *least*. Adverbs that have more than one syllable or that end in -ly use the word *more* to form the comparative, and the word *most* to form the superlative.

Comparative: The sun is closer to Earth than any other star.
We play soccer more frequently than baseball.
Superlative: The sun is the closest star to Earth.
Of all the sports to play, we play soccer most frequently.

Write in the blank the missing form of the adverb.

Adverb	Comparative	Superlative
1. fast	faster	fastest
2. high	higher	highest
3. soon	sooner	soonest
4. carefully	more carefully	most carefully
5. long	longer	longest
6. regularly	more regularly	most regularly
7. far	farther	farthest

Underline the correct form of the adverb in parentheses.

8. Jonathan always eats (faster, fastest) than his brother does.
9. We go swimming (more often, oftener) now that the weather is warmer.
10. Carlos wins (more frequently, most frequently) than his brother Eduardo.
11. The owl can screech the (louder, loudest) of all the birds that I know.
12. Samantha will arrive (sooner, soonest) of the 12 guests.
13. Lauren sat (closer, closest) to the exit door than Debbie did.
14. Jennifer is studying (more long, longer) than usual because she has a test tomorrow.
15. Senator Roberts speaks the (intelligentliest, most intelligently) of all the candidates.

---

page 121

Pictures Are Worth a Thousand Words

Comic strips tell a story in a short sequence of sketches and possibly a few short captions or conversation bubbles. Think of the most exciting experience in your life so far. Write the story. Then break the story into sequential steps. You have six cells to tell your story. Remember: cell one sets the story, and cell six is the conclusion; therefore, you are left with four cells to give the highlights of the event. The artistic merit of the drawings is not as important as the clarity of the story you tell.

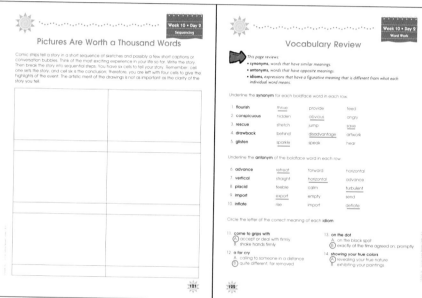

---

page 122

Vocabulary Review

This page reviews:
- **synonyms**, words that have similar meanings.
- **antonyms**, words that have opposite meanings.
- **idioms**, expressions that have a figurative meaning that is different from what each individual word means.

Underline the **synonym** for each boldface word in each row.

1. **flourish** — thrive — provide — feed
2. **conspicuous** — hidden — obvious — angry
3. **rescue** — stretch — jump — save
4. **drawback** — behind — disadvantage — artwork
5. **glisten** — sparkle — speak — hear

Underline the **antonym** of the boldface word in each row.

6. **advance** — retreat — forward — horizontal
7. **vertical** — straight — horizontal — advance
8. **placid** — feeble — calm — turbulent
9. **import** — export — empty — send
10. **inflate** — rise — import — deflate

Circle the letter of the correct meaning of each **idiom**.

11. come to grips with
Ⓐ accept or deal with firmly
B. shake hands firmly

12. a far cry
A. calling to someone in a distance
Ⓑ quite different; far removed

13. on the dot
A. on the black spot
Ⓑ exactly at the time agreed on; promptly

14. showing your true colors
Ⓐ revealing your true nature
B. exhibiting your paintings

---

page 123

Algebra Word Problems

Read these word problems carefully. Then, solve them using algebra. Show your work.

1. Right now, Jamal's mother is 3 times older than Jamal. But in 12 years, her age will be exactly 2 times greater than Jamal's. How old are Jamal and his mother today?

12, 36

2. Uncle Rupert asked Rachel to visit his farm to help count all the llamas and ostriches. The animals are running around really fast, but she's still sure she counted 35 heads and 94 feet. How many llamas are there? How many ostriches are there?

12 llamas; 23 ostriches

3. Larissa has a bag full of gumdrops. She knows there are fewer than 75 pieces of candy in all. When she divides them into groups of 3, 4, 5, or 6, there is always 1 gumdrop left over. How many gumdrops does Larissa have?

61 gumdrops

4. The sum of the ages of the three Perez sisters is 50. Rosa is the youngest, Elena is the middle sister, and Felicia is the oldest—10 years older than Rosa. Five years ago, their ages were prime numbers. How old was each then?

7, 11, 17

5. A pen and a pencil together cost $5.10. The pen costs $5 more than the pencil. How much does each cost?

$5 pen; 10¢ pencil

6. In the basketball league Ivy belongs to, 2 points are awarded for every shot made and 3 points are deducted for every shot missed. In one game, Ivy took 40 shots but scored 0 points. How many shots did she make? How many did she miss?

24; 16

7. Luisa noticed that in 7 years she'll be half her mother's age. If 3 years ago Luisa was ⅓ her mother's age, how old is her mother now?

33 years old

8. Kevin can do a job in 4 hours. It takes Kendra 2 hours to do the same job. If they do the job together, how long will it take them?

1⅓ hours

---

page 124

Troublesome Verbs

There are four verbs that often create problems for many writers: lay and lie, set and sit.

The verb **lay** *means to place.*
Examples: George, please lay the towels on the bathroom shelves. (present)
Joey laid the tile floor last week. (past)
Thomas has laid the two library books on the counter. (past participle)

The verb **lie** *means to recline.*
Examples: My baby sister lies in her crib until she awakes. (present)
As a child, I lay down for a nap every afternoon. (past)
The gifts have lain on the kitchen table since yesterday. (past participle)

Circle the best answer in the parentheses.

1. The cat likes to (lay, lie) near the warm stove.
2. The tile installers have (laid, lain) the floor to the patio.
3. Please (lay, lie) your essay on the desk when you have finished.
4. (Lay, Lie) the plastic cups and plates on the picnic table.

The verb **sit** *means to be in a seat or to rest.*
Examples: Kenny sits in the third row at the ball game. (present)
Kenny sat in the third row before (past)
Kenny has sat in the third row often. (past participle)

The verb **set** *means to put or place something.*
Examples: Lauren sets the plates on the table. (present)
Lauren set the plates on the table yesterday. (past)
Lauren has set the plates on the table since she was a young girl. (past participle)

Circle the best answer in the parentheses.

5. No one may (sit, set) on the patio while it is raining.
6. Please carefully (sit, set) the expensive vase on the dining room table.
7. Janie had (sat, set) the vase there many times.
8. Our next door neighbors (sit, set) with us during the concert.

---

page 125

The Art of Deception

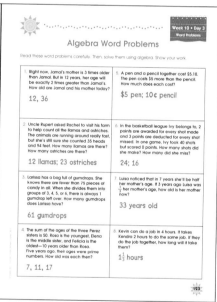

A beautiful but poisonous lion fish glides past. Wait, or is it a sea snake? Or a flat sole fish slipping down across the sand? There is an animal that can look like all of these creatures, and more.

The mimic octopus was discovered in 1998 in a river in Indonesia. It grows to about two feet in length and normally is striped white and brown. However, as its common name suggests, the mimic octopus changes its shape, color, and behavior to mimic, or appear like, other animals. This adaptation has developed over time to help the animal protect itself from predators.

While some other octopuses camouflage themselves, changing their color to blend into their environment, the mimic octopus changes its color and behavior to resemble dangerous animals. This represents a risky strategy for the octopus, instead of remaining safely hidden it must actively swim out and hope that its performance is good enough to fool predators. This form of mimicry, where a harmless species mimics a dangerous species, is called **Batesian mimicry**.

What Makes the Mimic Octopus Special?

Although many animals use mimicry to survive, the mimic octopus is the first known species to mimic several different animals.

This talented octopus has three confirmed impersonations: the lion fish, the sea snake, and the sole fish. To impersonate a poisonous lion fish, it floats above the sea floor, spreading its arms wide to resemble the lion fish's fins. For a sea snake impersonation, the octopus color shifts to the red and black bands associated with the venomous snake and wriggles two arms in different directions. To create the illusion of a toxic sole fish, it pulls its arms together into a heart shape, uses jet propulsion to build up speed, and undulates across the sea floor. The mimic octopus is also believed to take on the form of sand anemones, mantis shrimp, stingrays, and jellyfish.

Another remarkable attribute of the mimic octopus is that it seems to know which creature to impersonate to scare off its current predator. This demonstrates the octopus's high intelligence. For instance, when a mimic octopus is attacked by a damselfish, it imitates a banded sea snake, one of the damselfish's known predators. By taking on the appearance of a known predator of its attacker, the octopus is more likely to scare off its attacker.

A Recent Discovery

Researchers had not previously discovered the mimic octopus because its habitat is not a very popular place for divers to explore. The muddy river bottom lacks the vibrant diversity of life available in areas like the coral reefs. However, the stark nature of the landscape may have produced the mimic octopus' unusual adaptation. Since there is nowhere to hide, the octopus must either retreat into the ground or pretend to be something else. Scientists speculate that there may be even more species of mimic octopuses left to discover in more murky river bottoms.

---

page 126

Answer the following questions that relate to the preceding passage.

1. Someone that mimics—
Ⓐ eats something that looks like itself
Ⓑ looks, acts, or sounds like someone or something else.
C. cannot blend in to their environment.
D. is afraid of something.

2. The mimic octopus lives—
A. in forests near orb weaver spiders.
B. in the coral reefs in Australia.
Ⓒ in murky river bottoms in Indonesia.
D. at the bottom of the Pacific Ocean.

3. The antonym of camouflage is—
Ⓐ reveal.
B. hide.
C. army.
D. civilian.

4. When not mimicking, the mimic octopus—
A. hisses like a snake.
B. turns completely black.
Ⓒ has white and brown stripes.
D. undulates like a sole fish.

5. Batesian mimicry is demonstrated when—
Ⓐ a harmless species mimics a harmful one.
B. two harmful species mimic each other.
C. a creature hides itself in the sand.
D. someone named Bates mimics you.

6. Another title for this story could be—
A. Orb Weaver Spiders and Other Mimics.
B. New Octopus Discovered in 1998.
Ⓒ The Mimic Octopus: Nature's Best Performer.
D. A Damselfish Attacks: A Sea Floor Survival Guide.

7. When a damselfish appears, a mimic octopus will usually—
A. imitate a flat sole fish.
Ⓑ imitate a banded sea snake.
C. camouflage itself among the sand.
D. run and hide.

8. The mimic octopus's behavior in Question 7 demonstrates—
A. the octopus's high level of intelligence.
B. a form of Batesian mimicry.
Ⓒ both A and B.
D. none of the above.

9. Three animals the mimic octopus imitates are—
Ⓐ the lion fish, sea snake, and sole fish
B. the lion fish, dormouse, and sole fish
C. are the lion fish, damsel fish, and orb weaver spider.
D. are the lion fish, jellyfish, and Monarch.

10. The mimic octopus's habitat is—
A. filled with verdant colors.
B. the coral reefs.
C. popular with scuba divers.
Ⓓ murky river bottoms.

11. The mimic octopus was only discovered in 1998 because—
A. the coral reefs are heavily protected.
B. it lives in a popular area for divers.
Ⓒ it lives in an unpopular area to explore.
D. it is so good at mimicry.

12. Extending the previous answer, the most likely place to discover new creatures is—
A. in coral reefs.
B. in popular areas.
Ⓒ in unpopular areas.
D. in areas with much mimicry.

For the Future

Future tense verbs *tell about action that hasn't happened yet. Use* **will** *with a verb to show future tense.*

Complete this poster for the Totally Terrific Talent Show. Use a different verb to tell what talent each performer will share.

Totally Terrific Talent Show

1. Mister Greene _____will be_____ your host for the evening.
2. To open the show, the Tempo Trio _____will sing_____ the "Star-Spangled Banner."
3. Next on the bill, Kiyoko Sato _____will dance_____ her experimental blend of ballet and hip-hop.
4. Gilbert Lopez _____will play_____ a classical guitar interlude.
5. Scoot up to the edge of your seat! The Amazing Sabarisi _____will perform_____ jaw-dropping magic tricks.
6. College roommates Bronwyn and Jessica _____will recite_____ original poetry.
7. So everyone leaves in a good mood, Freddy Funniman _____will tell_____ the most hilarious jokes in his repertoire!
8. You _____will have_____ the best time in your life!

"Gr.8" Expectations

As the summer winds down and the new school year approaches, it is an excellent time to think about eighth grade expectations. Write a letter to yourself about what you hope to accomplish during the upcoming school year.

Be sure to think about social, athletic, maturational, and life goals as well as strictly academic ones.

_____

_____

_____

_____

_____

_____

_____

_____

_____

_____

_____

_____

_____

_____

_____

_____

THIS CERTIFIES THAT

IS NOW READY

FOR GRADE

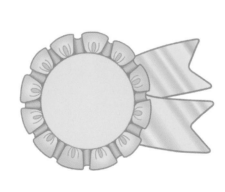

CONGRATULATIONS!

I'm proud of you!